AF560153

GENETICS AND HEREDITY

GENETICS
AND
HEREDITY

By

Dr. M. Prakash

Dept. of Zoology
M.M.H. Post Graduate College
Ghaziabad (U.P.)
(India)

DISCOVERY PUBLISHING HOUSE PVT. LTD.
NEW DELHI-110 002

Published by:
Tilak Wasan

DISCOVERY PUBLISHING HOUSE PVT. LTD.
4383/4B, Ansari Road, Darya Ganj
New Delhi-110 002 (India)
Phone : +91-11-23279245, 43596064-65
Fax : +91-11-23253475
E-mail : discoverypublishinghouse@gmail.com
sales@discoverypublishinggroup.com
web : www.discoverypublishinggroup.com

First Published: 2012

Reprinted: 2018

ISBN: 978-93-5056-086-0

Genetics and Heredity

Printed at:
Infinity Imaging Systems
Delhi

Preface

Genetics is the study of genes, and tries to explain what they are and how they work. Genes are how living organisms inherit features from their ancestors; for example, children usually look like their parents because they have inherited their parents' genes. Genetics tries to identify which features are inherited, and explain how these features are passed from generation to generation.

In genetics, a feature of a living thing is called a 'trait'. Some traits are part of an organism's physical appearance; such as a person's eye-colour, height or weight. Other sorts of traits are not easily seen and include blood types or resistance to diseases. Some traits are inherited through our genes, so tall and thin people tend to have tall and thin children. Other traits come from interactions between our genes and the environment, so a child might inherit the tendency to be tall, but if they are poorly nourished, they will still be short. The way our genes and environment interact to produce a trait can be complicated. For example, the chances of somebody dying of cancer or heart disease seems to depend on both their genes and their lifestyle.

Genes are made from a long molecule called DNA, which is copied and inherited across generations. DNA is made of simple units that line up in a particular order within this large molecule. The order of these units carries genetic information, similar to how the order of letters on a page carry information. The language used by DNA is called the genetic code, which lets organisms read the information in the genes. This information is the instructions for constructing and operating a living organism.

The information within a particular gene is not always exactly the same between one organism and another, so different copies of a gene do not always give exactly the same instructions. Each unique form of a single gene is called an allele. As an example, one allele for the gene for hair colour could instruct the body to produce a lot of pigment, producing black hair, while a different allele of the same gene might give garbled instructions that fail to produce any pigment, giving white hair. Mutations are random changes in genes, and can create new alleles. Mutations can also produce new traits, such as when mutations to an allele for black hair produce a new allele for white hair. This appearance of new traits is important in evolution.

Author

Contents

CHAPTER 1 Introduction

Genetics is the study of genes, and tries to explain what they are and how they work. Genes are how living organisms inherit features from their ancestors; for example, children usually look like their parents because they have inherited their parents' genes. Genetics tries to identify which features are inherited, and explain how these features are passed from generation to generation.

In genetics, a feature of a living thing is called a 'trait'. Some traits are part of an organism's physical appearance; such as a person's eye-colour, height or weight. Other sorts of traits are not easily seen and include blood types or resistance to diseases. Some traits are inherited through our genes, so tall and thin people tend to have tall and thin children. Other traits come from interactions between our genes and the environment, so a child might inherit the tendency to be tall, but if they are poorly nourished, they will still be short. The way our genes and environment interact to produce a trait can be complicated. For example, the chances of somebody dying of cancer or heart disease seems to depend on both their genes and their lifestyle.

Genes are made from a long molecule called DNA, which is copied and inherited across generations. DNA is made of simple units that line up in a particular order within this large molecule. The order of these units carries genetic information, similar to how the order of letters on a page carry information. The language used by DNA is called the genetic code, which lets organisms read the information in the genes. This information is the instructions for constructing and operating a living organism.

The information within a particular gene is not always exactly the same between one organism and another, so different copies of a gene do not always give exactly the same instructions. Each unique form of a single gene is called an allele. As an example, one allele for the gene for hair colour could instruct the body to produce a lot of pigment, producing black hair, while a different allele of the same gene might give garbled instructions that fail to produce any pigment, giving white hair. Mutations are random changes in genes, and can create new alleles. Mutations can also produce new traits, such as when mutations to an allele for black hair produce a new allele for white hair. This appearance of new traits is important in evolution.

Genes are inherited as units, with two parents dividing out copies of their genes to their offspring. You can think of this process like mixing two hands of cards, shuffling them, and then dealing them out again. Humans have two copies of each of their genes (*i.e.,* two alleles) and when people reproduce they make copies of their genes and put them into eggs or sperm, but only put in one copy of each type of gene. When an egg joins with a sperm, this gives a child a complete set of genes. This child will have the same number of genes as its parents, but for any gene one of their two copies will come from their father, and one from their mother.

The effects of this mixing depends on the types (the alleles) of the gene you are interested in. If the father has two alleles for green eyes, and the mother has two alleles for brown eyes, all their children will get two alleles that give different instructions, one for green eyes and one for brown.

The eye colour of these children depends on how these alleles work together. If one allele overrides the instructions from another, it is called the *dominant* allele, and the allele that is overridden is called the *recessive* allele. In the case of a daughter with both green and brown alleles, brown is dominant and she ends up with brown eyes.

Although the green colour allele is still there in this brown-eyed girl, it doesn't show. This is a difference between what you see on the surface (the traits of an organism, called its phenotype) and the genes within the organism (its genotype). In this example you can call the brown allele 'B' and the green allele 'g'. (It is normal to write dominant alleles with capital letters and recessive ones with lower-case letters.) The brown-eyed daughter has the 'brown eye phenotype' but her genotype is *Bg*, with one copy of the *B* allele, and one of the *g* allele.

Now imagine that this woman grows up and has children with a brown-eyed man who also has a *Bg* genotype. Her eggs will be a mixture of two types, one sort containing the *B* allele, and one sort the *g* allele. Similarly, her partner will produce a mix of two types of sperm containing one or the other of these two alleles. Now, when the alleles are mixed up in their offspring, these children have a chance of getting either brown or green eyes, since they could get a genotype of *BB* = brown eyes, *Bg* = brown eyes or *gg* = green eyes. In this generation, there is therefore a chance of the recessive allele showing itself in the phenotype of the children — some of them may have green eyes like their grandfather.

Many traits are inherited in a more complicated way than the example above. This can happen when there are several genes involved, each contributing a small part to the end result. Tall people tend to have tall children because their children get a package of many alleles that each contribute a bit to how much they grow. However, there are not clear groups of 'short people' and 'tall people', like there are groups of people with brown or green eyes. This is because of the large number of genes involved; this makes the trait very variable and people are of many different heights. Inheritance can also be complicated when the trait depends on the interaction between genetics and the environment. This is quite common, for example, if a child does not eat enough nutritious food this will not change traits like eye colour, but it could stunt their growth.

Inherited Diseases

Some diseases are hereditary and run in families; others, such as infectious diseases, are caused by the environment. Other diseases come from a combination of genes and the environment. Genetic disorders are diseases that are caused by a single allele of a gene and are inherited in families. These include Huntington's disease, Cystic fibrosis or Duchenne muscular dystrophy. Cystic fibrosis, for example, is caused by mutations in a single gene called *CFTR* and is inherited as a recessive trait.

Other diseases are influenced by genetics, but the genes a person gets from their parents only change their risk of getting a disease. Most of these diseases are inherited in a complex way, with either multiple genes involved, or coming from both genes and the environment. As an example, the risk of breast cancer is 50 times higher in the families most at risk, compared to the families least at risk. This variation is probably due to a large number of alleles, each changing the risk a little bit. Several of the genes have been identified, such as *BRCA1* and *BRCA2*, but not all of them. However, although some of the risk is genetic, the risk of this cancer is also increased by being overweight, drinking a lot of alcohol and not exercising. A woman's risk of breast cancer therefore comes from a large number of alleles interacting with her environment, so it is very hard to predict.

Genes Make Proteins

The function of genes is to provide the information needed to make molecules called proteins in cells. Cells are the smallest independent parts of organisms: the human body contains about 100 trillion cells, while very small organisms like bacteria are just one single cell. A cell is like a miniature and very complex factory that can make all the parts needed to produce a copy of itself, which happens when cells divide. There is a simple division of labour in cells – genes give instructions and proteins carry out these instructions, tasks like building a new copy of a cell, or repairing damage. Each type of protein is a specialist that only does one job, so if a cell needs to do something new, it must make a new protein to do this job. Similarly, if a cell needs to do something faster or slower than before, it makes more or less of the protein responsible. Genes tell cells what to do by telling them which proteins to make and in what amounts.

Proteins are made of a chain of 20 different types of amino acid molecules. This chain folds up into a compact shape, rather like an untidy ball of string. The shape of the protein is determined by the sequence of amino acids along its chain and it is this shape that, in turn, determines what the protein will do. For example, some proteins have parts of their surface that perfectly match the shape of another molecule, allowing the protein to bind to this molecule very tightly. Other proteins are enzymes, which are like tiny machines that alter other molecules.

The information in DNA is held in the sequence of the repeating units along the DNA chain. These units are four types of nucleotides (*A, T, G* and *C*) and the sequence of nucleotides stores information in an alphabet called the genetic code. When a gene is read by a cell the DNA sequence is copied into a very similar molecule called RNA (this process is called transcription). Transcription is controlled by other DNA sequences (such as promoters), which show a cell where genes are, and control how often they are copied. The RNA copy made from a gene is then fed through a structure called a ribosome, which translates the sequence of nucleotides in the RNA into the correct sequence of amino acids and joins these amino acids together to make a complete protein chain. The new protein then folds up into its active form. The process of moving information from the language of DNA into the language of amino acids is called translation.

If the sequence of the nucleotides in a gene changes, the sequence of the amino acids in the protein it produces may also change – if part of a gene is deleted, the protein produced will be shorter and may not work any more. This is the reason why different alleles of a gene can have different effects in an organism. As an example, hair colour depends on how much of a dark substance called melanin is put into the hair as it grows. If a person has a normal set of the genes involved in making melanin, they make all the proteins needed and they grow dark hair. However, if the alleles for a particular protein have different sequences and produce proteins that can't do their jobs, no melanin will be produced and the hair will be white. This condition is called albinism and the person with this condition is called an albino.

Genes are Copied

Genes are copied each time a cell divides into two new cells. The process that copies DNA is called DNA replication. It is through a similar process that a child inherits genes from its parents, when a copy from the mother is mixed with a copy from the father.

DNA can be copied very easily and accurately because each piece of DNA can direct the creation of a new copy of its information. This is because DNA is made of two strands that pair together like the two sides of a zipper. The nucleotides are in the centre, like the teeth in the zipper, and pair up to hold the two strands together. Importantly, the four different sorts of nucleotides are different shapes, so in order for the strands to close up properly, an *A* nucleotide must go opposite a *T* nucleotide, and a *G* opposite a *C*. This exact pairing is called base pairing.

When DNA is copied, the two strands of the old DNA are pulled apart by enzymes which move along each of the two single strands pairing up new nucleotide units and then zipping the strands closed. This produces two new pieces of DNA, each containing one strand from the old DNA and one newly made strand. This process isn't perfect and sometimes the proteins will make mistakes and put the wrong nucleotide into the strand they are building. This causes a change in the sequence of that gene. These changes in DNA sequence are called mutations. Mutations produce new alleles of genes. Sometimes these changes stop the gene from working properly, like the melanin genes discussed above. In other cases these mutations can change what the gene does or even let it do its job a little better than before. These mutations and their effects on the traits of organisms are one of the causes of evolution.

A population of organisms evolves when an inherited trait becomes more common or less common over time. For instance, all the mice living on an island would be a single population of mice. If over a few generations, white mice went from being rare, to being a large part of this population, then the coat colour of these mice would be evolving. In terms of genetics, this is called a change in allele frequency—such as an increase in the frequency of the allele for white fur.

Alleles become more or less common either just by chance (in a process called genetic drift), or through natural selection. In natural selection, if an allele makes it more likely that an organism will survive and reproduce, then over time this allele will become more common. But if an allele is harmful, natural selection will make it less common. For example, if the island was getting colder each year and was covered with snow for much of the time, then the allele for white fur would become useful for the mice, since it would make them harder to see against the snow. Fewer of the white mice would be eaten by predators, so over time white mice would out-compete mice with dark fur. White fur alleles would become more common, and dark fur alleles would become more rare.

Mutations create new alleles. These alleles have new DNA sequences and can produce proteins with new properties. So if an island was populated entirely by black mice, mutations could happen creating alleles for white fur. The combination of mutations creating new alleles at random, and natural selection picking out those which are useful, causes adaptation. This is when organisms change in ways that help them to survive and reproduce.

Since traits come from the genes in a cell, putting a new piece of DNA into a cell can produce a new trait. This is how genetic engineering works. For example, crop plants can be given a gene from an Arctic fish, so they produce an antifreeze protein in their leaves. This can help prevent frost damage. Other genes that can be put into crops include a natural insecticide from the bacteria *Bacillus thuringiensis*. The insecticide kills insects that eat the plants, but is harmless to people. In these plants the new genes are put into the plant before it is grown, so the genes will be in every part of the plant, including its seeds. The plant's offspring will then inherit the new genes, something which has led to concern about the spread of new traits into wild plants.

The kind of technology used in genetic engineering is also being developed to treat people with genetic disorders in an experimental medical technique called gene therapy. However, here the new gene is put in after the person has grown up and become ill, so any new gene will not be inherited by their children. Gene therapy works by trying to replace the allele that causes the disease with an allele that will work properly.

Genetics (from Ancient Greek *genetikos*, 'genitive' and that from *genesis*, 'origin', a discipline of biology, is the science of genes, heredity, and variation in living organisms. The fact that living things inherit traits from their parents has been used since prehistoric times to improve crop plants and animals through selective breeding. However, the modern science of genetics, which seeks to understand the process of inheritance, only began with the work of Gregor Mendel in the mid-19th century. Although he did not know the physical basis for heredity, Mendel observed that organisms inherit traits via discrete units of inheritance, which are now called genes.

Genes correspond to regions within DNA, a molecule composed of a chain of four different types of nucleotides–the sequence of these nucleotides is the genetic information organisms inherit. DNA naturally occurs in a double stranded form, with nucleotides on each strand complementary to each other. Each strand can act as a template for creating a new partner strand—this is the physical method for making copies of genes that can be inherited.

The sequence of nucleotides in a gene is translated by cells to produce a chain of amino acids, creating proteins—the order of amino acids in a protein corresponds to the order of nucleotides in the gene. This relationship between nucleotide sequence and amino acid sequence is known as the genetic code. The amino acids in a protein determine how it folds into a three-dimensional shape; this structure is, in turn, responsible for the protein's function. Proteins carry out almost all the functions needed for cells to live. A change to the DNA in a gene can change a protein's amino acids, changing its shape and function: this can have a dramatic effect in the cell and on the organism as a whole.

Although genetics plays a large role in the appearance and behaviour of organisms, it is the combination of genetics with what an organism experiences that determines the ultimate outcome. For example, while genes play a role in determining an organism's size, the nutrition and other conditions it experiences after inception also have a large effect.

Although the science of genetics began with the applied and theoretical work of Gregor Mendel in the mid-19th century, other theories of inheritance preceded Mendel. A popular theory during Mendel's time was the concept of blending inheritance: the idea that individuals inherit a smooth blend of traits from their parents. Mendel's work disproved this, showing that traits are composed of combinations of distinct genes rather than a continuous blend. Another theory that had some support at that time was the inheritance of acquired characteristics: the belief that individuals inherit traits strengthened by their parents. This theory (commonly associated with Jean-Baptiste Lamarck) is now known to be wrong—the experiences of individuals do not affect the genes they pass to their children. Other theories included the pangenesis of Charles Darwin (which had both acquired and inherited aspects) and Francis Galton's reformulation of pangenesis as both particulate and inherited.

The modern science of genetics traces its roots to Gregor Johann Mendel, a German-Czech Augustinian monk and scientist who studied the nature of inheritance in plants. In his paper 'Versuche über Pflanzenhybriden' ('Experiments on Plant Hybridization'), presented in 1865 to the *Naturforschender Verein* (Society for Research in Nature) in Brünn, Mendel traced the inheritance patterns of certain traits in pea plants and described them mathematically. Although this pattern of inheritance could only be observed for a few traits, Mendel's work suggested that heredity was particulate, not acquired, and that the inheritance patterns of many traits could be explained through simple rules and ratios.

The importance of Mendel's work did not gain wide understanding until the 1890s, after his death, when other scientists working on similar problems re-discovered his research. William Bateson, a proponent of Mendel's work, coined the word *genetics* in 1905. (The adjective *genetic*, derived from the Greek word *genesis*—, 'origin' and that from the word *genno*—, "to give birth", predates the noun and was first used in a biological sense in 1860.) Bateson popularized the usage of the word *genetics* to describe the study of inheritance in his inaugural address to the Third International Conference on Plant Hybridization in London, England, in 1906.

After the rediscovery of Mendel's work, scientists tried to determine which molecules in the cell were responsible for inheritance. In 1910, Thomas Hunt Morgan argued that genes are on chromosomes, based on observations of a sex-linked white eye mutation in fruit flies. In 1913, his student Alfred Sturtevant used the phenomenon of genetic linkage to show that genes are arranged linearly on the chromosome.

Although genes were known to exist on chromosomes, chromosomes are composed of both protein and DNA—scientists did not know which of these is responsible for inheritance. In 1928, Frederick Griffith discovered the phenomenon of transformation: dead bacteria could transfer genetic material to 'transform' other still-living bacteria. Sixteen years later, in 1944, Oswald Theodore Avery, Colin McLeod and Maclyn McCarty identified the molecule responsible for transformation as DNA. The Hershey-Chase experiment in 1952 also showed that DNA (rather than protein) is the genetic material of the viruses that infect bacteria, providing further evidence that DNA is the molecule responsible for inheritance.

James D. Watson and Francis Crick determined the structure of DNA in 1953, using the X-ray crystallography work of Rosalind Franklin and Maurice Wilkins that indicated DNA had a helical structure (i.e., shaped like a corkscrew). Their double-helix model had two strands of DNA with the nucleotides pointing inward, each matching a complementary nucleotide on the other strand to form what looks like rungs on a twisted ladder. This structure showed that genetic information exists in the sequence of nucleotides on each strand of DNA. The structure also suggested a simple method for duplication: if the strands are separated, new partner strands can be reconstructed for each based on the sequence of the old strand.

Although the structure of DNA showed how inheritance works, it was still not known how DNA influences the behaviour of cells. In the following years, scientists tried to understand how DNA controls the process of protein production. It was discovered that the cell uses DNA as a template to create matching messenger RNA (a molecule with nucleotides, very similar to DNA). The nucleotide sequence of a messenger RNA is used to create an amino acid sequence in protein; this translation between nucleotide and amino acid sequences is known as the genetic code.

With this molecular understanding of inheritance, an explosion of research became possible. One important development was chain-termination DNA sequencing in 1977 by Frederick Sanger. This technology allows scientists to read the nucleotide sequence of a DNA molecule. In 1983, Kary Banks Mullis developed the polymerase chain reaction, providing a quick way to isolate and amplify a specific section of a DNA from a mixture. Through the pooled efforts of the Human Genome Project and the parallel private effort by Celera Genomics, these and other techniques culminated in the sequencing of the human genome in 2003.

At its most fundamental level, inheritance in organisms occurs by means of discrete traits, called genes. This property was first observed by Gregor Mendel, who studied the segregation of heritable traits in pea plants. In his experiments studying the trait for flower colour, Mendel observed that the flowers of each pea plant were either purple or white—but never an intermediate between the two colours. These different, discrete versions of the same gene are called alleles.

In the case of pea, which is a diploid species, each individual plant has two alleles of each gene, one allele inherited from each parent. Many species, including humans, have this pattern of inheritance. Diploid organisms with two copies of the same allele of a given gene are called homozygous at that gene locus, while organisms with two different alleles of a given gene are called heterozygous.

The set of alleles for a given organism is called its genotype, while the observable traits of the organism are called its phenotype. When organisms are heterozygous at a gene, often one allele is called dominant as its qualities dominate the phenotype of the organism, while the other allele is called recessive as its qualities recede and are not observed. Some alleles do not have complete dominance and instead have incomplete dominance by expressing an intermediate phenotype, or codominance by expressing both alleles at once.

When a pair of organisms reproduce sexually, their offspring randomly inherit one of the two alleles from each parent. These observations of discrete inheritance and the segregation of alleles are collectively known as Mendel's first law or the Law of Segregation.

Geneticists use diagrams and symbols to describe inheritance. A gene is represented by one or a few letters. Often a '+' symbol is used to mark the usual, non-mutant allele for a gene.

In fertilization and breeding experiments (and especially when discussing Mendel's laws) the parents are referred to as the *'P'* generation and the offspring as the *'F1'* (first filial) generation. When the F1 offspring mate with each other, the offspring are called the *'F2'* (second filial) generation. One of the common diagrams used to predict the result of cross-breeding is the Punnett square.

When studying human genetic diseases, geneticists often use pedigree charts to represent the inheritance of traits. These charts map the inheritance of a trait in a family tree.

Human height is a complex genetic trait. Francis Galton's data from 1889 shows the relationship between offspring height as a function of mean parent height. While correlated, remaining variation in offspring heights indicates environment is also an important factor in this trait.

Organisms have thousands of genes, and in sexually reproducing organisms these genes generally assort independently of each other. This means that the inheritance of an allele for yellow or green pea colour is unrelated to the inheritance of alleles for white or purple flowers. This phenomenon, known as 'Mendel's second law' or the 'Law of independent assortment', means that the alleles of different genes get shuffled between parents to form offspring with many different combinations.

Often different genes can interact in a way that influences the same trait. In the Blue-eyed Mary (*Omphalodes verna*), for example, there exists a gene with alleles that determine the colour of flowers: blue or magenta. Another gene, however, controls whether the flowers have colour at all or are white. When a plant has two copies of this white allele, its flowers are white—regardless of whether the first gene has blue or magenta alleles. This interaction between genes is called epistasis, with the second gene epistatic to the first.

Many traits are not discrete features (e.g. purple or white flowers) but are instead continuous features (e.g. human height and skin colour). These complex traits are products of many genes. The influence of these genes is mediated, to varying degrees, by the environment an organism has experienced. The degree to which an organism's genes contribute to a complex trait is called heritability. Measurement of the heritability of a trait is relative—in a more variable environment, the environment has a bigger influence on the total variation of the trait. For example, human height is a complex trait with a heritability of 89 per cent in the United States. In Nigeria, however, where people experience a more variable access to good nutrition and health care, height has a heritability of only 62 per cent.

The molecular basis for genes is deoxyribonucleic acid (DNA). DNA is composed of a chain of nucleotides, of which there are four types: adenine (*A*), cytosine (*C*), guanine (*G*), and thymine (*T*). Genetic information exists in the sequence of these nucleotides, and genes exist as stretches of sequence along the DNA chain. Viruses are the only exception to this rule—sometimes viruses use the very similar molecule RNA instead of DNA as their genetic material.

DNA normally exists as a double-stranded molecule, coiled into the shape of a double-helix. Each nucleotide in DNA preferentially pairs with its partner nucleotide on the opposite strand: *A* pairs with *T*, and *C* pairs with *G*. Thus, in its two-stranded form, each strand effectively contains all necessary information, redundant with its partner strand. This structure of DNA is the physical basis for inheritance: DNA replication duplicates the genetic information by splitting the strands and using each strand as a template for synthesis of a new partner strand.

Genes are arranged linearly along long chains of DNA sequence, called chromosomes. In bacteria, each cell usually contains a single circular chromosome, while eukaryotic organisms (including plants and animals) have their DNA arranged in multiple linear chromosomes. These DNA strands are often extremely long; the largest human chromosome, for example, is about 247 million base pairs in length. The DNA of a chromosome is associated with structural proteins that organize, compact, and control access to the DNA, forming a material called chromatin; in eukaryotes, chromatin is usually composed of nucleosomes, segments of DNA wound around cores of histone proteins. The full set of hereditary material in an organism (usually the combined DNA sequences of all chromosomes) is called the genome.

While haploid organisms have only one copy of each chromosome, most animals and many plants are diploid, containing two of each chromosome and thus two copies of every gene. The two alleles for a gene are located on identical loci of sister chromatids, each allele inherited from a different parent.

An exception exists in the sex chromosomes, specialized chromosomes many animals have evolved that play a role in determining the sex of an organism. In humans and other mammals, the *Y* chromosome has very few genes and triggers the development of male sexual characteristics, while the *X* chromosome is similar to the other chromosomes and contains many genes unrelated to sex determination. Females have two copies of the *X* chromosome, but males have one *Y* and only one *X* chromosome; this difference in *X* chromosome copy numbers leads to the unusual inheritance patterns of sex-linked disorders.

When cells divide, their full genome is copied and each daughter cell inherits one copy. This process, called mitosis, is the simplest form of reproduction and is the basis for asexual reproduction. Asexual reproduction can also occur in multicellular organisms, producing offspring that inherit their genome from a single parent. Offspring that are genetically identical to their parents are called clones.

Eukaryotic organisms often use sexual reproduction to generate offspring that contain a mixture of genetic material inherited from two different parents. The process of sexual reproduction alternates between forms that contain single copies of the genome (haploid) and double copies (diploid). Haploid cells fuse and combine genetic material to create a diploid cell with paired chromosomes. Diploid organisms form haploids by dividing, without replicating their DNA, to create daughter cells that randomly inherit one of each pair of chromosomes. Most animals and many plants are diploid for most of their lifespan, with the haploid form reduced to single cell gametes such as sperm or eggs.

Although they do not use the haploid/diploid method of sexual reproduction, bacteria have many methods of acquiring new genetic information. Some bacteria can undergo conjugation, transferring a small circular piece of DNA to another bacterium. Bacteria can also take up raw DNA fragments found in the environment and integrate them into their genomes, a phenomenon known as transformation. These processes result in horizontal gene transfer, transmitting fragments of genetic information between organisms that would be otherwise unrelated.

The diploid nature of chromosomes allows for genes on different chromosomes to assort independently during sexual reproduction, recombining to form new combinations of genes. Genes on the same chromosome would theoretically never recombine, however, were it not for the process of chromosomal crossover. During crossover, chromosomes exchange stretches of DNA, effectively shuffling the gene alleles between the chromosomes. This process of chromosomal crossover generally occurs during meiosis, a series of cell divisions that creates haploid cells.

The probability of chromosomal crossover occurring between two given points on the chromosome is related to the distance between the points. For an arbitrarily long distance, the probability of crossover is high enough that the inheritance of the genes is effectively uncorrelated. For genes that are closer together, however, the lower probability of crossover means that the genes demonstrate genetic linkage—alleles for the two genes tend to be inherited together. The amounts of linkage between a series of genes can be combined to form a linear linkage map that roughly describes the arrangement of the genes along the chromosome.

Genes generally express their functional effect through the production of proteins, which are complex molecules responsible for most functions in the cell. Proteins are chains of amino acids, and the DNA sequence of a gene (through an RNA intermediate) is used to produce a specific protein sequence. This process begins with the production of an RNA molecule with a sequence matching the gene's DNA sequence, a process called transcription.

This messenger RNA molecule is then used to produce a corresponding amino acid sequence through a process called translation. Each group of three nucleotides in the sequence, called a codon, corresponds to one of the twenty possible amino acids in protein; this correspondence is called the genetic code. The flow of information is unidirectional: information is transferred from nucleotide sequences into the amino acid sequence of proteins, but it never transfers from protein back into the sequence of DNA—a phenomenon Francis Crick called the central dogma of molecular biology.

The specific sequence of amino acids results in a unique three-dimensional structure for that protein, and the three-dimensional structures of proteins are related to their functions. Some are simple structural molecules, like the fibres formed by the protein collagen. Proteins can bind to other proteins and simple molecules, sometimes acting as enzymes by facilitating chemical reactions within the bound molecules (without changing the structure of the protein itself). Protein structure is dynamic; the protein haemoglobin bends into slightly different forms as it facilitates the capture, transport, and release of oxygen molecules within mammalian blood.

A single nucleotide difference within DNA can cause a change in the amino acid sequence of a protein. Because protein structures are the result of their amino acid sequences, some changes can dramatically change the properties of a protein by destabilizing the structure or changing the surface of the protein in a way that changes its interaction with other proteins and molecules. For example, sickle-cell anaemia is a human genetic disease that results from a single base difference within the coding region for the ß-globin section of haemoglobin, causing a single amino acid change that changes haemoglobin's physical properties. Sickle-cell versions of haemoglobin stick to themselves, stacking to form fibres that distort the shape of red blood cells carrying the protein. These sickle-shaped cells no longer flow smoothly through blood vessels, having a tendency to clog or degrade, causing the medical problems associated with this disease.

Some genes are transcribed into RNA but are not translated into protein products—such RNA molecules are called non-coding RNA. In some cases, these products fold into structures which are involved in critical cell functions (e.g. ribosomal RNA and transfer RNA). RNA can also have regulatory effect through hybridization interactions with other RNA molecules (e.g. microRNA).

Although genes contain all the information an organism uses to function, the environment plays an important role in determining the ultimate phenotype—a phenomenon often referred to as 'nature *vs.* nurture'. The phenotype of an organism depends on the interaction of genetics with the environment. One example of this is the case of temperature-sensitive mutations. Often, a single amino acid change within the sequence of a protein does not change its behaviour and interactions with other molecules, but it does destabilize the structure. In a high temperature environment, where molecules are moving more quickly and hitting each other, this results in the protein losing its structure and failing to function. In a low temperature environment, however, the protein's structure is stable and it functions normally. This type of mutation is visible in the coat colouration of Siamese cats, where a mutation in an enzyme responsible for pigment production causes it to destabilize and lose function at high temperatures. The protein remains functional in areas of skin that are colder—legs, ears, tail, and face—and so the cat has dark fur at its extremities.

Environment also plays a dramatic role in effects of the human genetic disease phenylketonuria. The mutation that causes phenylketonuria disrupts the ability of the body to break down the amino acid phenylalanine, causing a toxic build-up of an intermediate molecule that, in turn, causes severe symptoms of progressive mental retardation and seizures. If someone with the phenylketonuria mutation follows a strict diet that avoids this amino acid, however, they remain normal and healthy.

A popular method to determine how much role nature and nurture play is to study identical and fraternal twins or siblings of multiple birth. Because identical siblings come from the same zygote they are genetically the same. Fraternal siblings however are as different genetically from one another as normal siblings. By comparing how often the twin of a set has the same disorder between fraternal and identical twins, scientists can see whether there is more of a nature or nurture effect. One famous example of a multiple birth study includes the Genain quadruplets, who were identical quadruplets all diagnosed with schizophrenia.

The genome of a given organism contains thousands of genes, but not all these genes need to be active at any given moment. A gene is expressed when it is being transcribed into mRNA (and translated into protein), and there exist many cellular methods of controlling the expression of genes such that proteins are produced only when needed by the cell. Transcription factors are regulatory proteins that bind to the start of genes, either promoting or inhibiting the transcription of the gene. Within the genome of *Escherichia coli* bacteria, for example, there exists a series of genes necessary for the synthesis of the amino acid tryptophan. However, when tryptophan is already available to the cell, these genes for tryptophan synthesis are no longer needed. The presence of tryptophan directly affects the activity of the genes–tryptophan molecules bind to the tryptophan repressor (a transcription factor), changing the repressor's structure such that the repressor binds to the genes. The tryptophan repressor blocks the transcription and expression of the genes, thereby creating negative feedback regulation of the tryptophan synthesis process.

Differences in gene expression are especially clear within multicellular organisms, where cells all contain the same genome but have very different structures and behaviours due to the expression of different sets of genes. All the cells in a multicellular organism derive from a single cell, differentiating into variant cell types in response to external and intercellular signals and gradually establishing different patterns of gene expression to create different behaviours. As no single gene is responsible for the development of structures within multicellular organisms, these patterns arise from the complex interactions between many cells.

Within eukaryotes there exist structural features of chromatin that influence the transcription of genes, often in the form of modifications to DNA and chromatin that are stably inherited by daughter cells. These features are called 'epigenetic' because they exist 'on top' of the DNA sequence and retain inheritance from one cell generation to the next. Because of epigenetic features, different cell types grown within the same medium can retain very different properties. Although epigenetic features are generally dynamic over the course of development, some, like the phenomenon of paramutation, have multigenerational inheritance and exist as rare exceptions to the general rule of DNA as the basis for inheritance.

During the process of DNA replication, errors occasionally occur in the polymerization of the second strand. These errors, called mutations, can have an impact on the phenotype of an organism, especially if they occur within the protein coding sequence of a gene. Error rates are usually very low—1 error in every 10-100 million bases—due to the 'proofreading' ability of DNA polymerases. (Without proofreading error rates are a thousand-fold higher; because many viruses rely on DNA and RNA polymerases that lack proofreading ability, they experience higher mutation rates.) Processes that increase the rate of changes in DNA are called mutagenic: mutagenic chemicals promote errors in DNA replication, often by interfering with the structure of base-pairing, while UV radiation induces mutations by causing damage to the DNA structure. Chemical damage to DNA occurs naturally as well, and cells use DNA repair mechanisms to repair mismatches and breaks in DNA—nevertheless, the repair sometimes fails to return the DNA to its original sequence.

In organisms that use chromosomal crossover to exchange DNA and recombine genes, errors in alignment during meiosis can also cause mutations. Errors in crossover are especially likely when similar sequences cause partner chromosomes to adopt a mistaken alignment; this makes some regions in genomes more prone to mutating in this way. These errors create large structural changes in DNA sequence—duplications, inversions or deletions of entire regions, or the accidental exchanging of whole parts between different chromosomes.

Mutations alter an organisms genotype and occasionally this causes different phenotypes to appear. Most mutations have little effect on an organism's phenotype, health, or reproductive fitness. Mutations that do have an effect are usually deleterious, but occasionally some can be beneficial. Studies in the fly *Drosophila melanogaster* suggest that if a mutation changes a protein produced by a gene, about 70 per cent of these mutations will be harmful with the remainder being either neutral or weakly beneficial.

Population genetics studies the distribution of genetic differences within populations and how these distributions change over time. Changes in the frequency of an allele in a population are mainly influenced by natural selection, where a given allele provides a selective or reproductive advantage to the organism, as well as other factors such as genetic drift, artificial selection and migration.

Over many generations, the genomes of organisms can change significantly, resulting in the phenomenon of evolution. Selection for beneficial mutations can cause a species to evolve into forms better able to survive in their environment, a process called adaptation. New species are formed through the process of speciation, often caused by geographical separations that prevent populations from exchanging genes with each other. The application of genetic principles to the study of population biology and evolution is referred to as the modern synthesis.

By comparing the homology between different species' genomes it is possible to calculate the evolutionary distance between them and when they may have diverged (called a molecular clock). Genetic comparisons are generally considered a more accurate method of characterizing the relatedness between species than the comparison of phenotypic characteristics. The evolutionary distances between species can be used to form evolutionary trees; these trees represent the common descent and divergence of species over time, although they do not show the transfer of genetic material between unrelated species (known as horizontal gene transfer and most common in bacteria).

Although geneticists originally studied inheritance in a wide range of organisms, researchers began to specialize in studying the genetics of a particular subset of organisms. The fact that significant research already existed for a given organism would encourage new researchers to choose it for further study, and so eventually a few model organisms became the basis for most genetics research. Common research topics in model organism genetics include the study of gene regulation and the involvement of genes in development and cancer.

Organisms were chosen, in part, for convenience—short generation times and easy genetic manipulation made some organisms popular genetics research tools. Widely used model organisms include the gut bacterium *Escherichia coli*, the plant *Arabidopsis thaliana*, baker's yeast (*Saccharomyces cerevisiae*), the nematode *Caenorhabditis elegans*, the common fruit fly (*Drosophila melanogaster*), and the common house mouse (*Mus musculus*).

Medical Genetics Research

Medical genetics seeks to understand how genetic variation relates to human health and disease. When searching for an unknown gene that may be involved in a disease, researchers commonly use genetic linkage and genetic pedigree charts to find the location on the genome associated with the disease. At the population level, researchers take advantage of Mendelian randomization to look for locations in the genome that are associated with diseases, a technique especially useful for multigenic traits not clearly defined by a single gene. Once a candidate gene is found, further research is often done on the corresponding gene (called an orthologous gene) in model organisms. In addition to studying genetic diseases, the increased availability of genotyping techniques has led to the field of pharmacogenetics–studying how genotype can affect drug responses.

Individuals differ in their inherited tendency to develop cancer, and cancer is a genetic disease. The process of cancer development in the body is a combination of events. Mutations occasionally occur within cells in the body as they divide. Although these mutations will not be inherited by any offspring, they can affect the behaviour of cells, sometimes causing them to grow and divide more frequently. There are biological mechanisms that attempt to stop this process; signals are given to inappropriately dividing cells that should trigger cell death, but sometimes additional mutations occur that cause cells to ignore these messages. An internal process of natural selection occurs within the body and eventually mutations accumulate within cells to promote their own growth, creating a cancerous tumour that grows and invades various tissues of the body.

Research Techniques

DNA can be manipulated in the laboratory. Restriction enzymes are commonly used enzymes that cut DNA at specific sequences, producing predictable fragments of DNA. DNA fragments can be visualized through use of gel electrophoresis, which separates fragments according to their length.

The use of ligation enzymes allows DNA fragments to be connected, and by ligating fragments of DNA together from different sources, researchers can create recombinant DNA. Often associated with genetically modified organisms, recombinant DNA is commonly used in the context of plasmids–short circular DNA fragments with a few genes on them. By inserting plasmids into bacteria and growing those bacteria on plates of agar (to isolate clones of bacteria cells), researchers can clonally amplify the inserted fragment of DNA (a process known as molecular cloning). (Cloning can also refer to the creation of clonal organisms, through various techniques.)

DNA can also be amplified using a procedure called the polymerase chain reaction (PCR). By using specific short sequences of DNA, PCR can isolate and exponentially amplify a targeted region of DNA. Because it can amplify from extremely small amounts of DNA, PCR is also often used to detect the presence of specific DNA sequences.

DNA Sequencing and Genomics

One of the most fundamental technologies developed to study genetics, DNA sequencing allows researchers to determine the sequence of nucleotides in DNA fragments. Developed in 1977 by Frederick Sanger and co-workers, chain-termination sequencing is now routinely used to sequence DNA fragments. With this technology, researchers have been able to study the molecular sequences associated with many human diseases.

As sequencing has become less expensive, researchers have sequenced the genomes of many organisms, using computational tools to stitch together the sequences of many different fragments (a process called genome assembly). These technologies were used to sequence the human genome, leading to the completion of the Human Genome Project in 2003. New high-throughput sequencing technologies are dramatically lowering the cost of DNA sequencing, with many researchers hoping to bring the cost of resequencing a human genome down to a thousand dollars.

The large amount of sequence data available has created the field of genomics, research that uses computational tools to search for and analyze patterns in the full genomes of organisms. Genomics can also be considered a subfield of bioinformatics, which uses computational approaches to analyze large sets of biological data.

History of Genetics

The history of genetics is generally held to have started with the work of an Augustinian friar, Gregor Mendel. Gregor Mendel is known as the father of genetics. His work on pea plants, published in 1866, described what came to be known as Mendelian Inheritance. In the centuries before—and for several decades after—Mendel's work, a wide variety of theories of heredity proliferated (*see below*). 1900 marked the 'rediscovery of Mendel' by Hugo de Vries, Carl Correns and Erich von Tschermak, and by 1915 the basic principles of Mendelian genetics had been applied to a wide variety of organisms—most notably the fruit fly *Drosophila melanogaster*. Led by Thomas Hunt Morgan and his fellow 'drosophilists', geneticists developed the Mendelian-chromosome theory of heredity, which was widely accepted by 1925. Alongside experimental work, mathematicians developed the statistical framework of population genetics, bring genetical explanations into the study of evolution.

With the basic patterns of genetic inheritance established, many biologists turned to investigations of the physical nature of the gene. In the 1940s and early 1950s, experiments pointed to DNA as the portion of chromosomes (and perhaps other nucleoproteins) that held genes. A focus on new model organisms such as viruses and bacteria, along with the discovery of the double helical structure of DNA in 1953, marked the transition to the era of molecular genetics. In the following years, chemists developed techniques for sequencing both nucleic acids and proteins, while others worked out the relationship between the two forms of biological molecules: the genetic code. The regulation of gene expression became a central issue in the 1960s; by the 1970s gene expression could be controlled and manipulated through genetic engineering. In the last decades of the 20th century, many biologists focussed on large-scale genetics projects, sequencing entire genomes.

The most influential early theories of heredity were that of Hippocrates and Aristotle. Hippocrates' theory (possibly based on the teachings of Anaxagoras) was similar to Darwin's later ideas on pangenesis, involving heredity material that collects from throughout the body. Aristotle suggested instead that the (nonphysical) form-giving principle of an organism was transmitted through semen (which he considered to be a purified form of blood) and the mother's menstrual blood, which interacted in the womb to direct an organism's early development. For both Hippocrates and Aristotle—and nearly all Western scholars through to the late 19th century—the inheritance of acquired characters was a supposedly well-established fact that any adequate theory of heredity had to explain. At the same time, individual species were taken to have a fixed essence; such inherited changes were merely superficial.

In the 9th century CE, the Afro-Arab writer Al-Jahiz considered the effects of the environment on the likelihood of an animal to survive, and first described the struggle for existence. His ideas on the struggle for existence in the *Book of Animals* have been summarized as follows:

> "Animals engage in a struggle for existence; for resources, to avoid being eaten and to breed. Environmental factors influence organisms to develop new

characteristics to ensure survival, thus transforming into new species. Animals that survive to breed can pass on their successful characteristics to offspring".

In 1000 CE, the Arab physician, Abu al-Qasim al-Zahrawi (known as Albucasis in the West), wrote the first clear description of haemophilia, a hereditary genetic disorder, in his *Al-Tasrif*. In this work, he wrote of an Andalusian family whose males died of bleeding after minor injuries.

Plant Systematics and Hybridization

In the 18th century, with increased knowledge of plant and animal diversity and the accompanying increased focus on taxonomy, new ideas about heredity began to appear. Linnaeus and others (among them Joseph Gottlieb Kölreuter, Carl Friedrich von Gärtner, and Charles Naudin) conducted extensive experiments with hybridization, especially species hybrids. Species hybridizers described a wide variety of inheritance phenomena, include hybrid sterility and the high variability of back-crosses.

Plant breeders were also developing an array of stable varieties in many important plant species. In the early 19th century, Augustin Sageret established the concept of dominance, recognizing that when some plant varieties are crossed, certain characters (present in one parent) usually appear in the offspring; he also found that some ancestral characters found in neither parent may appear in offspring. However, plant breeders made little attempt to establish a theoretical foundation for their work or to share their knowledge with current work of physiology.

Post-Mendel, Pre-re-discovery

Mendel's work was published in a relatively obscure scientific journal, and it was not given any attention in the scientific community. Instead, discussions about modes of heredity were galvanized by Darwin's theory of evolution by natural selection, in which mechanisms of non-Lamarckian heredity seemed to be required. Darwin's own theory of heredity, pangenesis, did not meet with any large degree of acceptance. A more mathematical version of pangenesis, one which dropped much of Darwin's Lamarckian holdovers, was developed as the "biometrical" school of heredity by Darwin's cousin, Francis Galton. Under Galton and his successor Karl Pearson, the biometrical school attempted to build statistical models for heredity and evolution, with some limited but real success, though the exact methods of heredity were unknown and largely unquestioned.

Classical Genetics

The significance of Mendel's work was not understood until early in the twentieth century, after his death, when his research was re-discovered by other scientists working on similar problems. Hugo de Vries, Carl Correns and Erich von Tschermak.

There was then a feud between Bateson and Pearson over the hereditary mechanism. Fisher solved this in the Correlation between Relatives on the Supposition of Mendelian Inheritance.

- 1865 Gregor Mendel's paper, *Experiments on Plant Hybridization.*
- 1869 Friedrich Miescher discovers a weak acid in the nuclei of white blood cells that today we call DNA
- 1880-1890 Walther Flemming, Eduard Strasburger, and Edouard van Beneden elucidate chromosome distribution during cell division.
- 1889 Hugo de Vries postulates that "inheritance of specific traits in organisms comes in particles", naming such particles '(pan)genes'.
- 1903 Walter Sutton hypothesizes that chromosomes, which segregate in a Mendelian fashion, are hereditary units.

- 1905 William Bateson coins the term 'genetics' in a letter to Adam Sedgwick and at a meeting in 1906.
- 1908 Hardy-Weinberg law derived.
- 1910 Thomas Hunt Morgan shows that genes reside on chromosomes.
- 1913 Alfred Sturtevant makes the first genetic map of a chromosome.
- 1913 Gene maps show chromosomes containing linear arranged genes.
- 1918 Ronald Fisher publishes "The Correlation Between Relatives on the Supposition of Mendelian Inheritance" the modern synthesis of genetics and evolutionary biology starts. (*See population genetics*).
- 1928 Frederick Griffith discovers that hereditary material from dead bacteria can be incorporated into live bacteria (*see Griffith's experiment*).
- 1931 Crossing over is identified as the cause of recombination.
- 1933 Jean Brachet is able to show that DNA is found in chromosomes and that RNA is present in the cytoplasm of all cells.
- 1941 Edward Lawrie Tatum and George Wells Beadle show that genes code for proteins; see the original central dogma of genetics.

The DNA Era

- 1944 The Avery–MacLeod–McCarty experiment isolates DNA as the genetic material (at that time called transforming principle)
- 1950 Erwin Chargaff shows that the four nucleotides are not present in nucleic acids in stable proportions, but that some general rules appear to hold (e.g., that the amount of adenine, *A*, tends to be equal to that of thymine, *T*).

Barbara McClintock discovers transposons in maize

- 1952 The Hershey-Chase experiment proves the genetic information of phages (and all other organisms) to be DNA
- 1953 DNA structure is resolved to be a double helix by James D. Watson and Francis Crick
- 1956 Joe Hin Tjio and Albert Levan established the correct chromosome number in humans to be 46
- 1958 The Meselson-Stahl experiment demonstrates that DNA is semi-conservatively replicated
- 1961-1967 Combined efforts of scientists 'crack' the genetic code, including Marshall Nirenberg, Har Gobind Khorana, Sydney Brenner & Francis Crick
- 1964 Howard Temin showed using RNA viruses that the direction of DNA to RNA transcription can be reversed.
- 1970 Restriction enzymes were discovered in studies of a bacterium, *Haemophilus influenzae,* enabling scientists to cut and paste DNA.

The Genomics Era

- 1972, Walter Fiers and his team at the Laboratory of Molecular Biology of the University of Ghent (Ghent, Belgium) were the first to determine the sequence of a gene: the gene for bacteriophage MS2 coat protein.
- 1976, Walter Fiers and his team determine the complete nucleotide-sequence of bacteriophage MS2-RNA.
- 1977 DNA is sequenced for the first time by Fred Sanger, Walter Gilbert, and Allan Maxam working independently. Sanger's lab sequence the entire genome of bacteriophage F-X174.
- 1983 Kary Banks Mullis discovers the polymerase chain reaction enabling the easy amplification of DNA.

- 1989 The human gene that encodes the CFTR protein was sequenced by Francis Collins and Lap-Chee Tsui. Defects in this gene cause cystic fibrosis.
- 1995 The genome of *Haemophilus influenzae* is the first genome of a free living organism to be sequenced.
- 1996 *Saccharomyces cerevisiae* is the first eukaryote genome sequence to be released.
- 1998 The first genome sequence for a multicellular eukaryote, *Caenorhabditis elegans*, is released.
- 2001 First draft sequences of the human genome are released simultaneously by the Human Genome Project and Celera Genomics.
- 2003 (14 April) Successful completion of Human Genome Project with 99 per cent of the genome sequenced to a 99.99 per cent accuracy.

Gregor Mendel

Gregor Johann Mendel was an Austrian Augustinian monk and scientist, who gained posthumous fame as the figurehead of the new science of genetics for his study of the inheritance of certain traits in pea plants. Mendel showed that the inheritance of these traits follows particular laws, which were later named after him. The significance of Mendel's work was not recognized until the turn of the 20th century. The independent rediscovery of these laws formed the foundation of the modern science of genetics.

Mendel was born into an ethnic German family in Heinzendorf bei Odrau, Austrian Silesia, Austrian Empire (now Hyncice, Czech Republic), and was baptized two days later. He was the son of Anton and Rosine Mendel, and had one older sister and one younger. They lived and worked on a farm which had been owned by the Mendel family for at least 130 years. During his childhood, Mendel worked as a gardener, studied beekeeping, and as a young man attended the Philosophical Institute in Olomouc in 1840-1843. Upon recommendation of his physics teacher Friedrich Franz, he entered the Augustinian Abbey of St Thomas in Brno in 1843. Born Johann Mendel, he took the name Gregor upon entering monastic life. In 1851 he was sent to the University of Vienna to study under the sponsorship of Abbot C.F. Napp. At Vienna, his professor of physics was Christian Doppler. Mendel returned to his abbey in 1853 as a teacher, principally of physics, and by 1867, he had replaced Napp as abbot of the monastery.

Besides his work on plant breeding while at St Thomas's Abbey, Mendel also bred bees in a bee house that was built for him, using bee hives that he designed. He also studied astronomy and meteorology, founding the 'Austrian Meteorological Society' in 1865. The majority of his published works were related to meteorology.

Experiments on Plant Hybridization

Gregor Mendel, who is known as the 'father of modern genetics', was inspired by both his professors at university and his colleagues at the monastery to study variation in plants, and he conducted his study in the monastery's two hectare experimental garden, which was originally planted by the abbot Napp in 1830. Between 1856 and 1863 Mendel cultivated and tested some 29,000 pea plants (*i.e., Pisum sativum*). This study showed that one in four pea plants had purebred recessive alleles, two out of four were hybrid and one out of four were purebred dominant. His experiments led him to make two generalizations, the Law of Segregation and the Law of Independent Assortment, which later became known as Mendel's Laws of Inheritance.

Mendel did read his paper, *Experiments on Plant Hybridization,* at two meetings of the Natural History Society of Brünn in Moravia in 1865. It was received favourably and generated reports in several local newspapers. When Mendel's paper was published in 1866 in *Proceedings of the Natural History Society of Brünn*, it was seen as essentially about hybridization rather than inheritance and had little impact and was cited about three times over the next thirty-five years. (Notably, Charles Darwin was unaware of Mendel's paper, according to Jacob Bronowski's *The Ascent of Man*.) His paper was criticized at the time, but is now considered a seminal work.

Life After the Pea Experiments

After Mendel completed his work with peas, he turned to experimenting with honeybees, in order to extend his work to animals. He produced a hybrid strain (so vicious they were destroyed), but failed to generate a clear picture of their heredity because of the difficulties in controlling mating behaviours of queen bees. He also described novel plant species, and these are denoted with the botanical author abbreviation 'Mendel'.

After he was elevated as abbot in 1868, his scientific work largely ended as Mendel became consumed with his increased administrative responsibilities, especially a dispute with the civil government over their attempt to impose special taxes on religious institutions. At first Mendel's work was rejected, and it was not widely accepted until after he died. At that time most biologists held the idea of blending inheritance, and Charles Darwin's efforts to explain inheritance through a theory of pangenesis were unsuccessful. Mendel's ideas were rediscovered in the early twentieth century, and in the 1930s and 1940s the modern synthesis combined Mendelian genetics with Darwin's theory of natural selection.

It was not until the early 20th century that the importance of his ideas was realized. By 1900, research aimed at finding a successful theory of discontinuous inheritance rather than blending inheritance led to independent duplication of his work by Hugo de Vries and Carl Correns, and the rediscovery of Mendel's writings and laws. Both acknowledged Mendel's priority, and it is thought probable that de Vries did not understand the results he had found until after reading Mendel. Though Erich von Tschermak was originally also credited with rediscovery, this is no longer accepted because he did not understand Mendel's laws. Though de Vries later lost interest in Mendelism, other biologists started to establish genetics as a science.

Mendel's results were quickly replicated, and genetic linkage quickly worked out. Biologists flocked to the theory, even though it was not yet applicable to many phenomena, it sought to give a genotypic understanding of heredity which they felt was lacking in previous studies of heredity which focussed on phenotypic approaches. Most prominent of these latter approaches was the biometric school of Karl Pearson and W.F.R. Weldon, which was based heavily on statistical studies of phenotype variation. The strongest opposition to this school came from William Bateson, who perhaps did the most in the early days of publicising the benefits of Mendel's theory (the word 'genetics', and much of the discipline's other terminology, originated with Bateson). This debate between the biometricians and the Mendelians was extremely vigorous in the first two decades of the twentieth century, with the biometricians claiming statistical and mathematical rigor, whereas the Mendelians claimed a better understanding of biology. In the end, the two approaches were combined as the modern synthesis of evolutionary biology, especially by work conducted by R. A. Fisher as early as 1918.

Mendel's experimental results have later been the object of considerable dispute. Fisher analyzed the results of the *F2* (second filial) ratio and found them to be implausibly close to the exact ratio of 3 to 1. Only a few would accuse Mendel of scientific malpractice or call it a scientific fraud—reproduction of his experiments has demonstrated the validity of his hypothesis—however, the results have continued to be a mystery for many, though it is often cited as an example of confirmation bias. This might arise if he detected an approximate 3 to 1 ratio early in his experiments with a small sample size, and continued collecting more data until the results conformed more nearly to an exact ratio. It is sometimes suggested that he may have censored his results, and that his seven traits each occur on a separate chromosome pair, an extremely unlikely occurrence if they were chosen at random. In fact, the genes Mendel studied occurred in only four linkage groups, and only one gene pair (out of 21 possible) is close enough to show deviation from independent assortment; this is not a pair that Mendel studied. Some recent researchers have suggested that Fisher's criticisms of Mendel's work may have been exaggerated.

CHAPTER 3

Gene

A gene is a unit of heredity in a living organism. It normally resides on a stretch of DNA that codes for a type of protein or for an RNA chain that has a function in the organism. All living things depend on genes, as they specify all proteins and functional RNA chains. Genes hold the information to build and maintain an organism's cells and pass genetic traits to offspring, although some organelles (e.g. mitochondria) are self-replicating and are not coded for by the organism's DNA.

A modern working definition of a gene is "*a locatable region of genomic sequence, corresponding to a unit of inheritance, which is associated with regulatory regions, transcribed regions, and or other functional sequence regions* ". Colloquial usage of the term *gene* (e.g. 'good genes', 'hair colour gene') may actually refer to an allele: a *gene* is the basic instruction, a sequence of nucleic acid (DNA or, in the case of certain viruses RNA), while an *allele* is one variant of that gene. Thus, when the mainstream press refers to 'having' a 'gene' for a specific trait, this may be incorrect. In many cases, all people would have the gene in question, but certain people will have a specific allele of that gene, which results in the trait. In the simplest case, the changes observed may be caused by a single letter of the genetic code — a single nucleotide polymorphism.

The notion of a gene is evolving with the science of genetics, which began when Gregor Mendel noticed that biological variations are inherited from parent organisms as specific, discrete traits. The biological entity responsible for defining traits was later termed a *gene*, but the biological basis for inheritance remained unknown until DNA was identified as the genetic material in the 1940s. All organisms have many genes corresponding to many different biological traits, some of which are immediately visible, such as eye colour or number of limbs, and some of which are not, such as blood type or increased risk for specific diseases, or the thousands of basic biochemical processes that comprise life.

The vast majority of living organisms encode their genes in long strands of DNA. DNA (deoxyribonucleic acid) consists of a chain made from four types of nucleotide subunits, each composed of: a five-carbon sugar (2'-deoxyribose), a phosphate group, and one of the four bases adenine, cytosine, guanine, and thymine. The most common form of DNA in a cell is in a double helix structure, in which two individual DNA strands twist around each other in a right-handed spiral. In this structure, the base pairing rules specify that guanine pairs with cytosine and adenine pairs with thymine. The base pairing between guanine and cytosine forms three hydrogen bonds, whereas the base pairing between adenine and thymine forms two hydrogen bonds. The two strands in a double helix must therefore be *complementary*, that is, their bases must align such that the adenines of one strand are paired with the thymines of the other strand, and so on.

Due to the chemical composition of the pentose residues of the bases, DNA strands have directionality. One end of a DNA polymer contains an exposed hydroxyl group on the deoxyribose; this is known as the 3′ end of the molecule. The other end contains an exposed phosphate group; this is the 5′ end. The directionality of DNA is vitally important to many cellular processes, since double helices are necessarily directional (a strand running 5′-3′ pairs with a complementary strand running 3′-5′), and processes such as DNA replication occur in only one direction. All nucleic acid synthesis in a cell occurs in the 5′-3′ direction, because new monomers are added via a dehydration reaction that uses the exposed 3′ hydroxyl as a nucleophile.

The expression of genes encoded in DNA begins by transcribing the gene into RNA, a second type of nucleic acid that is very similar to DNA, but whose monomers contain the sugar ribose rather than deoxyribose. RNA also contains the base uracil in place of thymine. RNA molecules are less stable than DNA and are typically single-stranded. Genes that encode proteins are composed of a series of three-nucleotide sequences called codons, which serve as the *words* in the genetic *language*. The genetic code specifies the correspondence during protein translation between codons and amino acids. The genetic code is nearly the same for all known organisms.

When proteins are manufactured, the gene is first copied into RNA as an intermediate product. In other cases, the RNA molecules are the actual functional products. For example, RNAs known as ribozymes are capable of enzymatic function, and microRNA has a regulatory role. The DNA sequences from which such RNAs are transcribed are known as RNA genes.

Some viruses store their entire genomes in the form of RNA, and contain no DNA at all. Because they use RNA to store genes, their cellular hosts may synthesize their proteins as soon as they are infected and without the delay in waiting for transcription. On the other hand, RNA retroviruses, such as HIV, require the reverse transcription of their genome from RNA into DNA before their proteins can be synthesized. In 2006, French researchers came across a puzzling example of RNA-mediated inheritance in mouse. Mice with a loss-of-function mutation in the gene Kit have white tails. Offspring of these mutants can have white tails despite having only normal Kit genes. The research team traced this effect back to mutated Kit RNA. While RNA is common as genetic storage material in viruses, in mammals in particular RNA inheritance has been observed very rarely.

Functional Structure of a Gene

All genes have regulatory regions in addition to regions that explicitly code for a protein or RNA product. A regulatory region shared by almost all genes is known as the promoter, which provides a position that is recognized by the transcription machinery when a gene is about to be transcribed and expressed. A gene can have more than one promoter, resulting in RNAs that differ in how far they extend in the 5' end. Although promoter regions have a consensus sequence that is the most common sequence at this position, some genes have 'strong' promoters that bind the transcription machinery well, and others have 'weak' promoters that bind poorly. These weak promoters usually permit a lower rate of transcription than the strong promoters, because the transcription machinery binds to them and initiates transcription less frequently. Other possible regulatory regions include enhancers, which can compensate for a weak promoter. Most regulatory regions are 'upstream'—that is, before or toward the 5' end of the transcription initiation site. Eukaryotic promoter regions are much more complex and difficult to identify than prokaryotic promoters.

Many prokaryotic genes are organized into operons, or groups of genes whose products have related functions and which are transcribed as a unit. By contrast, eukaryotic genes are transcribed only one at a time, but may include long stretches of DNA called introns which are transcribed but never translated into protein (they are spliced out before translation). Splicing can also occur in prokaryotic genes, but is less common than in eukaryotes.

The total complement of genes in an organism or cell is known as its genome, which may be stored on one or more chromosomes; the region of the chromosome at which a particular gene is located is called its locus. A chromosome consists of a single, very long DNA helix on which thousands of genes are encoded. Prokaryotes—bacteria and archaea—typically store their genomes on a single large, circular chromosome, sometimes supplemented by additional small circles of DNA called plasmids, which usually encode only a few genes and are easily transferable between individuals. For example, the genes for antibiotic resistance are usually encoded on bacterial plasmids and can be passed between individual cells, even those of different species, via horizontal gene transfer. Although some simple eukaryotes also possess plasmids with small numbers of genes, the majority of eukaryotic genes are stored on multiple linear chromosomes, which are packed within the nucleus in complex with storage proteins called histones. The manner in which DNA is stored on the histone, as well as chemical modifications of the histone itself, are regulatory mechanisms governing whether a particular region of DNA is accessible for gene expression. The ends of eukaryotic chromosomes are capped by long stretches of repetitive sequences called telomeres, which do not code for any gene product but are present to prevent degradation of coding and regulatory regions during DNA replication. The length of the telomeres tends to decrease each time the genome is replicated in preparation for cell division; the loss of telomeres has been proposed as an explanation for cellular senescence, or the loss of the ability to divide, and by extension for the aging process in organisms.

Whereas the chromosomes of prokaryotes are relatively gene-dense, those of eukaryotes often contain so-called 'junk DNA', or regions of DNA that serve no obvious function. Simple single-celled eukaryotes have relatively small amounts of such DNA, whereas the genomes of complex multicellular organisms, including humans, contain an absolute majority of DNA without an identified function. However it now appears that, although protein-coding DNA makes up barely

2 per cent of the human genome, about 80 per cent of the bases in the genome may be being expressed, so the term 'junk DNA' may be a misnomer.

In all organisms, there are two major steps separating a protein-coding gene from its protein: First, the DNA on which the gene resides must be *transcribed* from DNA to messenger RNA (mRNA); and, second, it must be *translated* from mRNA to protein. RNA-coding genes must still go through the first step, but are not translated into protein. The process of producing a biologically functional molecule of either RNA or protein is called gene expression, and the resulting molecule itself is called a gene product.

Genetic Code

The genetic code is the set of rules by which a gene is translated into a functional protein. Each gene consists of a specific sequence of nucleotides encoded in a DNA (or sometimes RNA) strand; a correspondence between nucleotides, the basic building blocks of genetic material, and amino acids, the basic building blocks of proteins, must be established for genes to be successfully translated into functional proteins. Sets of three nucleotides, known as codons, each correspond to a specific amino acid or to a signal; three codons are known as 'stop codons' and, instead of specifying a new amino acid, alert the translation machinery that the end of the gene has been reached. There are 64 possible codons (four possible nucleotides at each of three positions, hence 4^3 possible codons) and only 20 standard amino acids; hence the code is redundant and multiple codons can specify the same amino acid. The correspondence between codons and amino acids is nearly universal among all known living organisms.

The process of genetic transcription produces a single-stranded RNA molecule known as messenger RNA, whose nucleotide sequence is complementary to the DNA from which it was transcribed. The DNA strand whose sequence matches that of the RNA is known as the coding strand and the strand from which the RNA was synthesized is the template strand. Transcription is performed by an enzyme called an RNA polymerase, which reads the template strand in the 3' to 5' direction and synthesizes the RNA from 5' to 3'. To initiate transcription, the polymerase first recognizes and binds a promoter region of the gene. Thus a major mechanism of gene regulation is the blocking or sequestering of the promoter region, either by tight binding by repressor molecules that physically block the polymerase, or by organizing the DNA so that the promoter region is not accessible.

In prokaryotes, transcription occurs in the cytoplasm; for very long transcripts, translation may begin at the 5′ end of the RNA while the 3′ end is still being transcribed. In eukaryotes, transcription necessarily occurs in the nucleus, where the cell's DNA is sequestered; the RNA molecule produced by the polymerase is known as the primary transcript and must undergo post-transcriptional modifications before being exported to the cytoplasm for translation. The splicing of introns present within the transcribed region is a modification unique to eukaryotes; alternative splicing mechanisms can result in mature transcripts from the same gene having different sequences and thus coding for different proteins. This is a major form of regulation in eukaryotic cells.

Translation is the process by which a mature mRNA molecule is used as a template for synthesizing a new protein. Translation is carried out by ribosomes, large complexes of RNA and protein responsible for carrying out the chemical reactions to add new amino acids to a growing polypeptide chain by the formation of peptide bonds. The genetic code is read three nucleotides at a time, in units called codons, via interactions with specialized RNA molecules called transfer RNA (tRNA). Each tRNA has three unpaired bases known as the anticodon that are complementary to the codon it reads; the tRNA is also covalently attached to the amino acid specified by the complementary codon. When the tRNA binds to its complementary codon in an mRNA strand, the ribosome ligates its amino acid cargo to the new polypeptide chain, which is synthesized from amino terminus to carboxyl terminus. During and after its synthesis, the new protein must fold to its active three-dimensional structure before it can carry out its cellular function.

DNA Replication and Inheritance

The growth, development, and reproduction of organisms relies on cell division, or the process by which a single cell divides into two usually identical daughter cells. This requires first making a duplicate copy of every gene in the genome in a process called DNA replication. The copies are made by specialized enzymes known as DNA polymerases, which 'read' one strand of the double-helical DNA, known as the template strand, and synthesize a new complementary strand. Because the DNA double helix is held together by base pairing, the sequence of one strand completely specifies the sequence of its complement; hence only one strand needs to be read by the enzyme to produce a faithful copy. The process of DNA replication is semiconservative; that is, the copy of the genome inherited by each daughter cell contains one original and one newly synthesized strand of DNA.

After DNA replication is complete, the cell must physically separate the two copies of the genome and divide into two distinct membrane-bound cells. In prokaryotes — bacteria and archaea — this usually occurs via a relatively simple process called binary fission, in which each circular genome attaches to the cell membrane and is separated into the daughter cells as the membrane invaginates to split the cytoplasm into two membrane-bound portions. Binary fission is extremely fast compared to the rates of cell division in eukaryotes. Eukaryotic cell division is a more complex process known as the cell cycle; DNA replication occurs during a phase of this cycle known as *S* phase, whereas the process of segregating chromosomes and splitting the cytoplasm occurs during *M* phase. In many single-celled eukaryotes such as yeast, reproduction by budding is common, which results in asymmetrical portions of cytoplasm in the two daughter cells.

Molecular Inheritance

The duplication and transmission of genetic material from one generation of cells to the next is the basis for molecular inheritance, and the link between the classical and molecular pictures of genes. Organisms inherit the characteristics of their parents because the cells of the offspring contain copies of the genes in their parents' cells. In asexually reproducing organisms, the offspring will be a genetic copy or clone of the parent organism. In sexually reproducing organisms, a specialized form of cell division called meiosis produces cells called gametes or germ cells that are haploid, or contain only one copy of each gene. The gametes produced by females are called eggs or ova, and those produced by males are called sperm. Two gametes fuse to form a fertilized egg, a single cell that once again has a diploid number of genes—each with one copy from the mother and one copy from the father.

During the process of meiotic cell division, an event called genetic recombination or *crossing-over* can sometimes occur, in which a length of DNA on one chromatid is swapped with a length of DNA on the corresponding sister chromatid. This has no effect if the alleles on the chromatids are the same, but results in reassortment of otherwise linked alleles if they are different. The Mendelian principle of independent assortment asserts that each of a parent's two genes for each trait will sort independently into gametes; which allele an organism inherits for one trait is unrelated to which allele it inherits for another trait. This is in fact only true for genes that do not reside on the same chromosome, or are located very far from one another on the same chromosome. The closer two genes lie on the same chromosome, the more closely they will be associated in gametes and the more often they will appear together; genes that are very close are essentially never separated because it is extremely unlikely that a crossover point will occur between them. This is known as genetic linkage.

History

Prior to Mendel's work, the dominant theory of heredity was one of blending inheritance, which proposes that the traits of the parents blend or mix in a smooth, continuous gradient in the offspring. Although Mendel's work was largely unrecognized after its first publication in 1866, it was rediscovered in 1900 by three European scientists, Hugo de Vries, Carl Correns, and Erich von Tschermak, who had reached similar conclusions from their own research. However, these scientists were not yet aware of the identity of the 'discrete units' on which genetic material resides.

The existence of genes was first suggested by Gregor Mendel (1822-1884), who, in the 1860s, studied inheritance in peaplants (*Pisum sativum*) and hypothesized a factor that conveys traits from parent to offspring. He spent over 10 years of his life on one experiment. Although he did not use the term *gene*, he explained his results in terms of inherited characteristics. Mendel was also the first to hypothesize independent assortment, the distinction between dominant and recessive traits, the distinction between a heterozygote and homozygote, and the difference between what would later be described as genotype (the genetic material of an organism) and phenotype (the visible traits of that organism). Mendel's concept was given a name by Hugo de Vries in 1889, who, at that time probably unaware of Mendel's work, in his book *Intracellular Pangenesis* coined the term 'pangen' for "the smallest particle [representing] one hereditary characteristic".

Darwin used the term Gemmule to describe a microscopic unit of inheritance, and what would later become known as Chromosomes had been observed separating out during cell division by Wilhelm Hofmeister as early as 1848. The idea that chromosomes are the carriers of inheritance was expressed in 1883 by Wilhelm Roux. The modern conception of the gene originated with work by Gregor Mendel, a 19th-century Augustinian monk who systematically studied heredity in pea plants. Mendel's work was the first to illustrate particulate inheritance, or the theory that inherited traits are passed from one generation to the next in discrete units that interact in well-defined ways. Danish botanist Wilhelm Johannsen coined the word 'gene' ('gen' in Danish and German) in 1909 to describe these fundamental physical and functional units of heredity, while the related word genetics was first used by William Bateson in 1905. The word was derived from Hugo de Vries' 1889 term *pangen* for the same concept, itself a derivative of the word *pangenesis* coined by Darwin (1868). The word pangenesis is made from the Greek words *pan* (a prefix meaning 'whole', 'encompassing') and *genesis* ('birth') or *genos* ('origin').

In the early 1900s, Mendel's work received renewed attention from scientists. In 1910, Thomas Hunt Morgan showed that genes reside on specific chromosomes. He later showed that genes occupy specific locations on the chromosome. With this knowledge, Morgan and his students began the first chromosomal map of the fruit fly *Drosophila.* In 1928, Frederick Griffith showed that genes could be transferred. In what is now known as Griffith's experiment, injections into a mouse of a deadly strain of bacteria that had been heat-killed transferred genetic information to a safe strain of the same bacteria, killing the mouse.

A series of subsequent discoveries led to the realization decades later that chromosomes within cells are the carriers of genetic material, and that they are made of DNA (deoxyribonucleic acid), a polymeric molecule found in all cells on which the 'discrete units' of Mendelian inheritance are encoded.

In 1941, George Wells Beadle and Edward Lawrie Tatum showed that mutations in genes caused errors in specific steps in metabolic pathways. This showed that specific genes code for specific proteins, leading to the 'one gene, one enzyme' hypothesis. Oswald Avery, Colin Munro MacLeod, and Maclyn McCarty showed in 1944 that DNA holds the gene's information. In 1953, James D. Watson and Francis Crick demonstrated the molecular structure of DNA. Together, these discoveries established the central dogma of molecular biology, which states that proteins are translated from RNA which is transcribed from DNA. This dogma has since been shown to have exceptions, such as reverse transcription in retroviruses.

In 1972, Walter Fiers and his team at the Laboratory of Molecular Biology of the University of Ghent (Ghent, Belgium) were the first to determine the sequence of a gene: the gene for Bacteriophage MS2 coat protein. Richard J. Roberts and Phillip Sharp discovered in 1977 that genes can be split into segments. This led to the idea that one gene can make several proteins. Recently (as of 2003-2006), biological results let the notion of gene appear more slippery. In particular, genes do not seem to sit side by side on DNA like discrete beads. Instead, regions of the DNA producing distinct proteins may overlap, so that the idea emerges that 'genes are one long continuum'.

It was first hypothesized in 1986 by Walter Gilbert that neither DNA nor protein would be required in such a primitive system as that of a very early stage of the earth if RNA could perform as simply a catalyst and genetic information storage processor.

The modern study of genetics at the level of DNA is known as molecular genetics and the synthesis of molecular genetics with traditional Darwinian evolution is known as the modern evolutionary synthesis.

According to the theory of Mendelian inheritance, variations in phenotype–the observable physical and behavioural characteristics of an organism–are due to variations in genotype, or the organism's particular set of genes, each of which specifies a particular trait. Different forms of a gene, which may give rise to different phenotypes, are known as alleles. Organisms such as the pea plants Mendel worked on, along with many plants and animals, have two alleles for each trait, one inherited from each parent. Alleles may be dominant or recessive; dominant alleles give rise to their corresponding phenotypes when paired with any other allele for the same trait, whereas recessive alleles give rise to their corresponding phenotype only when paired with another copy of the same allele. For example, if the allele specifying tall stems in pea plants is dominant over the allele specifying short stems, then pea plants that inherit one tall allele from one parent and one short allele from the other parent will also have tall stems. Mendel's work found that alleles assort independently in the production of gametes, or germ cells, ensuring variation in the next generation.

Mutation

DNA replication is for the most part extremely accurate, with an error rate per site of around 10^{-6} to 10^{-10} in eukaryotes. Rare, spontaneous alterations in the base sequence of a particular gene arise from a number of sources, such as errors in DNA replication and the aftermath of DNA damage. These errors are called mutations. The cell contains many DNA repair mechanisms for preventing mutations and maintaining the integrity of the genome; however, in some cases—such as breaks in both DNA strands of a chromosome—repairing the physical damage to the molecule is a higher priority than producing an exact copy. Due to the degeneracy of the genetic code, some mutations in protein-coding genes are *silent*, or produce no change in the amino acid sequence of the protein for which they code; for example, the codons UCU and UUC both code for serine, so the U?C mutation has no effect on the protein. Mutations that do have phenotypic effects are most often neutral or deleterious to the organism, but sometimes they confer benefits to the organism's fitness.

Mutations propagated to the next generation lead to variations within a species' population. Variants of a single gene are known as alleles, and differences in alleles may give rise to differences in traits. Although it is rare for the variants in a single gene to have clearly distinguishable phenotypic effects, certain well-defined traits are in fact controlled by single genetic loci. A gene's most common allele is called the wild type allele, and rare alleles are called mutants. However, this does not imply that the wild-type allele is the ancestor from which the mutants are descended.

Chromosomal Organization

The total complement of genes in an organism or cell is known as its genome. In prokaryotes, the vast majority of genes are located on a single chromosome of circular DNA, while eukaryotes usually possess multiple individual linear DNA helices packed into dense DNA-protein complexes called chromosomes. Genes that appear together on one chromosome of one species may appear on separate chromosomes in another species. Many species carry more than one copy of their genome within each of their somatic cells. Cells or organisms with only one copy of each chromosome are called haploid; those with two copies are called diploid; and those with more than two copies are called polyploid. The copies of genes on the chromosomes are not necessarily identical. In sexually reproducing organisms, one copy is normally inherited from each parent.

Number of Genes

Early estimates of the number of human genes that used expressed sequence tag data put it at 50 000-100 000. Following the sequencing of the human genome and other genomes, it has been found that rather few genes (~20 000 in human, mouse and fly, ~13 000 in roundworm, >46 000 in rice) encode all the proteins in an organism. These protein-coding sequences make up 1-2 per cent of the human genome. A large part of the genome is transcribed however, to introns, retrotransposons and seemingly a large array of non-coding RNAs. Total number of proteins (the Earth's proteome) is estimated to be 5 million sequences.

Genetic and Genomic Nomenclature

Gene nomenclature has been established by the HUGO Gene Nomenclature Committee (HGNC) for each known human gene in the form of an approved gene name and symbol (short-form abbreviation). All approved symbols are stored in the HGNC Database. Each symbol is unique and each gene is only given one approved gene symbol. This also facilitates electronic data retrieval from publications. In preference each symbol maintains parallel construction in different members of a gene family and can be used in other species, especially the mouse.

Evolutionary Concept of a Gene

George C. Williams first explicitly advocated the gene-centric view of evolution in his 1966 book *Adaptation and Natural Selection*. He proposed an evolutionary concept of gene to be used when we are talking about natural selection favouring some genes. The definition is: "that which segregates and recombines with appreciable frequency." According to this definition, even an asexual genome could be considered a gene, insofar that it have an appreciable permanency through many generations.

The difference is: the molecular gene *transcribes* as a unit, and the evolutionary gene *inherits* as a unit.

Richard Dawkins' books *The Selfish Gene* (1976) and *The Extended Phenotype* (1982) defended the idea that the gene is the only replicator in living systems. This means that only genes transmit their structure largely intact and are potentially immortal in the form of copies. So, genes should be the unit of selection. In *The Selfish Gene* Dawkins attempts to redefine the word 'gene' to mean "an inheritable unit" instead of the generally accepted definition of "a section of DNA coding for a particular protein". In *River Out of Eden,* Dawkins further refined the idea of gene-centric selection by describing life as a river of compatible genes flowing through geological time. Scoop up a bucket of genes from the river of genes, and we have an organism serving as temporary bodies or survival machines. A river of genes may fork into two branches representing two non-interbreeding species as a result of geographical separation.

Gene Targeting and Implications

Gene targeting is commonly referred to techniques for altering or disrupting mouse genes and provides the mouse models for studying the roles of individual genes in embryonic development, human disorders, aging and diseases. The mouse models, where one or more of its genes are deactivated or made inoperable, are called knockout mice. Since the first reports in which homologous recombination in embryonic stem cells was used to generate gene-targeted mice, gene targeting has proven to be a powerful means of precisely manipulating the mammalian genome, producing at least ten thousand mutant mouse strains and it is now possible to introduce mutations that can be activated at specific time points, or in specific cells or organs, both during development and in the adult animal.

Gene targeting strategies have been expanded to all kinds of modifications, including point mutations, isoform deletions, mutant allele correction, large pieces of chromosomal DNA insertion and deletion, tissue specific disruption combined with spatial and temporal regulation and so on. It is predicted that the ability to generate mouse models with predictable phenotypes will have a major impact on studies of all phases of development, immunology, neurobiology, oncology, physiology, metabolism, and human diseases. Gene targeting is also in theory applicable to species from which totipotent embryonic stem cells can be established, and therefore may offer a potential to the improvement of domestic animals and plants.

Changing Concept

The concept of the gene has changed considerably (*see history section*). From the original definition of a 'unit of inheritance', the term evolved to mean a DNA-based unit that can exert its effects on the organism through RNA or protein products. It was also previously believed that one gene makes one protein; this concept was overthrown by the discovery of alternative splicing and trans-splicing.

The definition of a gene is still changing. The first cases of RNA-based inheritance have been discovered in mammals. Evidence is also accumulating that the control regions of a gene do not necessarily have to be close to the coding sequence on the linear molecule or even on the same chromosome. Spilianakis and colleagues discovered that the promoter region of the interferon-gamma gene on chromosome 10 and the regulatory regions of the T(H)2 cytokine locus on chromosome 11 come into close proximity in the nucleus possibly to be jointly regulated.

The concept that genes are clearly delimited is also being eroded. There is evidence for fused proteins stemming from two adjacent genes that can produce two separate protein products. While it is not clear whether these fusion proteins are functional, the phenomenon is more frequent than previously thought. Even more ground-breaking than the discovery of fused genes is the observation that some proteins can be composed of exons from far away regions and even different chromosomes. This new data has led to an updated, and probably tentative, definition of a gene as "a union of genomic sequences encoding a coherent set of potentially overlapping functional products." This new definition categorizes genes by functional products, whether they be proteins or RNA, rather than specific DNA loci; all regulatory elements of DNA are therefore classified as *gene-associated* regions.

Gene Expression

Gene expression is the process by which information from a gene is used in the synthesis of a functional gene product. These products are often proteins, but in non-protein coding genes such as rRNA genes or tRNA genes, the product is a functional RNA. The process of gene expression is used by all known life-eukaryotes (including multicellular organisms), prokaryotes (bacteria and archaea) and viruses — to generate the macromolecular machinery for life. Several steps in the gene expression process may be modulated, including the transcription, RNA splicing, translation, and post-translational modification of a protein. Gene regulation gives the cell control over structure and function, and is the basis for cellular differentiation, morphogenesis and the versatility and adaptability of any organism. Gene regulation may also serve as a substrate for evolutionary change, since control of the timing, location, and amount of gene expression can have a profound effect on the functions (actions) of the gene in a cell or in a multicellular organism.

In genetics, gene expression is the most fundamental level at which genotype gives rise to the phenotype. The genetic code is 'interpreted' by gene expression, and the properties of the expression products give rise to the organism's phenotype.

RNA Processing

Transcription of protein encoding genes creates a primary transcript of RNA at the place where the gene was located. This transcript can be altered before being translated, this is particularly common in eukaryotes. The most common RNA processing is splicing to remove introns. Introns are RNA segments which are not found in the mature RNA, although they can function as precursors, e.g. for snoRNAs, which are RNAs that direct modification of nucleotides in other RNAs. Introns are common in eukaryotic genes but rare in prokaryotes.

RNA processing, also known as post-transcriptional modification, can start during transcription, as is the case for splicing, where the spliceosome removes introns from newly formed RNA.

Extensive RNA processing may be an evolutionary advantage made possible by the nucleus of eukaryotes. In prokaryotes transcription and translation happen together whilst in eukaryotes the nuclear membrane separates the two processes giving time for RNA processing to occur.

Non-coding RNA Maturation

In most organisms non-coding genes (ncRNA) are transcribed as precursors which undergo further processing. In the case of ribosomal RNAs (rRNA), they are often transcribed as a pre-rRNA which contains one or more rRNAs, the pre-rRNA is cleaved and modified (2'-O-methylation and pseudouridine formation) at a specific sites by approximately 150 different small nucleolus-restricted RNA species, called small nucleolar RNAs(snoRNAs) , which like snRNAs, snoRNAs associate with proteins, forming snoRNPs. In eukaryotes, in particular a snoRNP, called RNase MRP cleaves the 45S pre-rRNA into the 28S, 5.8S, and 18S rRNAs. The rRNA and RNA processing factors are form large aggregates called the nucleolus. In the case of transfer RNA (tRNA), for example, the 5' sequence is removed by RNase P, whereas the 3' end is removed by the tRNase Z enzyme. In the case of micro RNA (miRNA), miRNAs are first transcribed as primary transcripts or pri-miRNA with a cap and poly-A tail and processed to short, 70-nucleotide stem-loop structures known as pre-miRNA in the cell nucleus by the enzymes Drosha and Pasha, after being exported, it is then processed to mature miRNAs in the cytoplasm by interaction with the endonuclease Dicer, which also initiates the formation of the RNA-induced silencing complex (RISC), composed of the Argonaute protein.

For some RNA (non-coding RNA) the mature RNA is the finished gene product. In the case of messenger RNA (mRNA) the RNA is an information carrier coding for the synthesis of one or more proteins. mRNA carrying a single protein sequence (common in eukaryotes) is monocistronic whilst mRNA carrying multiple protein sequences (common in prokaryotes) is known as polycistronic.

Each triplet of nucleotides of the coding regions of a messenger RNA corresponds to a binding site for a transfer RNA. Transfer RNAs carry amino acids, and these are chained together by the ribosome. The ribosome helps transfer RNA to bind to messenger RNA and takes the amino acid from each transfer RNA and makes a structure-less protein out of it. In prokaryotes translation generally occurs at the point of transcription, often using a messenger RNA which is still in the process of being created. In eukaryotes translation can occur in a variety of regions of the cell depending on where the protein being written is supposed to be. Major locations are the cytoplasm for soluble cytoplasmic proteins and the endoplasmic reticulum for proteins which are for export from the cell or insertion into a cell membrane. Proteins which are supposed to be expressed at the endoplasmic reticulum are recognised part-way through the translation process. This is governed by the signal recognition particle - a protein which binds to the ribosome and directs it to the endoplasmic reticulum when it finds a signal sequence on the growing (nascent) amino acid chain.

Protein Transport

Many proteins are destined for other parts of the cell than the cytosol and a wide range of signalling sequences are used to direct proteins to where they are supposed to be. In prokaryotes this is normally a simple process due to limited compartmentalisation of the cell. However in eukaryotes there is a great variety of different targeting processes to ensure the protein arrives at the correct organelle.

Not all proteins remain within the cell and many are exported, for example digestive enzymes, hormones and extracellular matrix proteins. In eukaryotes the export pathway is well developed and the main mechanism for the export of these proteins is translocation to the endoplasmatic reticulum, followed by transport via the Golgi apparatus.

Measurement

Measuring gene expression is an important part of many life sciences — the ability to quantify the level at which a particular gene is expressed within a cell, tissue or organism can give a huge amount of information. For example measuring gene expression can:

- ❖ Identify viral infection of a cell (viral protein expression)
- ❖ Determine an individual's susceptibility to cancer (oncogene expression)
- ❖ Find if a bacterium is resistant to penicillin (beta-lactamase expression)

Similarly the analysis of the location of expression protein is a powerful tool and this can be done on an organism or cellular scale. Investigation of localisation is particularly important for study of development in multicellular organisms and as an indicator of protein function in single cells. Ideally measurement of expression is done by detecting the final gene product (for many genes this is the protein) however it is often easier to detect one of the precursors, typically mRNA, and infer gene expression level.

mRNA Quantification

Levels of mRNA can be quantitatively measured by Northern blotting which gives size and sequence information about the mRNA molecules. A sample of RNA is separated on an agarose gel and hybridized to a radio-labelled RNA probe that is complementary to the target sequence. The radio-labelled RNA is then detected by an autoradiograph. The main problems with Northern blotting stem from the use of radioactive reagents (which make the procedure time consuming and potentially dangerous) and lower quality quantification than more modern methods (due to the fact that quantification is done by measuring band strength in an image of a gel). Northern blotting is, however, still widely used as the additional mRNA size information allows the discrimination of alternately spliced transcripts.

A more modern low-throughput approach for measuring mRNA abundance is reverse transcription quantitative polymerase chain reaction (RT-PCR followed with qPCR). RT-PCR first generates a DNA template from the mRNA by reverse transcription, which is called cDNA. This cDNA template is then used for qPCR where the change in fluorescence of a probe changes as the DNA amplification process progresses. With a carefully constructed standard curve qPCR can produce an absolute measurement such as number of copies of mRNA, typically in units of copies per nanolitre of homogenized tissue or copies per cell. qPCR is very sensitive (detection of a single mRNA molecule is possible), but can be expensive due to the fluorescent probes required.

Northern blots and RT-qPCR are good for detecting whether a single gene is being expressed, but it quickly becomes impractical if many genes within the sample are being studied. Using DNA microarrays transcript levels for many genes at once (expression profiling) can be measured. Recent advances in microarray technology allow for the quantification, on a single array, of transcript levels for every known gene in several organism's genomes, including humans.

Alternatively 'tag based' technologies like Serial analysis of gene expression (SAGE), which can provide a relative measure of the cellular concentration of different messenger RNAs, can be used. The great advantage of tag-based methods is the 'open architecture', allowing for the exact measurement of any transcript, with a known or unknown sequence.

Protein Quantification

For genes encoding proteins the expression level can be directly assessed by a number of means with some clear analogies to the techniques for mRNA quantification.

The most commonly used method is to perform a Western blot against the protein of interest — this gives information on the size of the protein in addition to its identity. A sample (often cellular lysate) is separated on a polyacrylamide gel, transferred to a membrane and then probed with an antibody to the protein of interest. The antibody can either be conjugated to a fluorophore or to horseradish peroxidase for imaging and/or quantification. The gel-based nature of this assay makes quantification less accurate but it has the advantage of being able to identify later modifications to the protein, for example proteolysis or ubiquitination, from changes in size.

By replacing the gene with a new version fused a green fluorescent protein (or similar) marker expression may be directly quantified in live cells. This is done by imaging using a fluorescence microscope. It is very difficult to clone a GFP-fused protein into its native location in the genome without affecting expression levels so this method often cannot be used to measure endogenous gene expression. It is, however, widely used to measure the expression of a gene artificially introduced into the cell, for example via an expression vector. It is important to note that by fusing a target protein to a fluorescent reporter the protein's behavior, including its cellular localization and expression level, can be significantly changed.

The enzyme-linked immunosorbent assay works by using antibodies immobilised on a microtiter plate to capture proteins of interest from samples added to the well. Using a detection antibody conjugated to an enzyme or fluorophore the quantity of bound protein can be accurately measured by fluorometric or colourimetric detection. The detection process is very similar to that of a Western blot, but by avoiding the gel steps more accurate quantification can be achieved.

Analysis of expression is not limited to only quantification; localisation can also be determined. mRNA can be detected with a suitably labelled complementary mRNA strand and protein can be detected via labelled antibodies. The probed sample is then observed by microscopy to identify where the mRNA or protein is.

Regulation of gene expression refers to the control of the amount and timing of appearance of the functional product of a gene. Control of expression is vital to allow a cell to produce the gene products it needs when it needs them; in turn this gives cells the flexibility to adapt to a variable environment, external signals, damage to the cell, etc. Some simple examples of where gene expression is important are:

- Control of Insulin expression so it gives a signal for blood glucose regulation.
- *X* chromosome inactivation in female mammals to prevent an 'overdose' of the genes it contains.
- Cyclin expression levels control progression through the eukaryotic cell cycle.

More generally gene regulation gives the cell control over all structure and function, and is the basis for cellular differentiation, morphogenesis and the versatility and adaptability of any organism.

Any step of gene expression may be modulated, from the DNA-RNA transcription step to post-translational modification of a protein. The stability of the final gene product, whether it is RNA or protein, also contributes to the expression level of the gene - an unstable product results in a low expression level. In general gene expression is regulated through changes in the number and type of interactions between molecules that collectively influence transcription of DNA and translation of RNA.

Numerous terms are used to describe types of genes depending on how they are regulated, these include:

- A constitutive gene is a gene that is transcribed continually compared to a facultative gene which is only transcribed when needed.
- A housekeeping gene is typically a constitutive gene that is transcribed at a relatively constant level. The housekeeping gene's products are typically needed for maintenance of the cell. It is generally assumed that their expression is unaffected by experimental conditions. Exmaples include actin, GAPDH and ubiquitin.
- A facultative gene is a gene which is only transcribed when needed compared to a constitutive gene.
- An inducible gene is a gene whose expression is either responsive to environmental change or dependent on the position in the cell cycle.

Transcriptional Regulation

Regulation of transcription can be broken down into three main routes of influence; genetic (direct interaction of a control factor with the gene), modulation (interaction of a control factor with the transcription machinery) and epigenetic (non-sequence changes in DNA structure which influence transcription).

Direct interaction with DNA is the simplest and most direct method a protein can change transcription levels and genes often have several protein binding sites around the coding region with the specific function of regulating transcription. There are many classes of regulatory DNA binding sites known as enhancers, insulators, repressors and silencers. The mechanisms for regulating transcription are very varied, from blocking key binding sites on the DNA for RNA polymerase to acting as an activator and promoting transcription by assisting RNA polymerase binding.

The activity of transcription factors is further modulated by intracellular signals causing protein post-translational modification including phosphorylated, acetylated, or glycosylated. These changes influence a transcription factor's ability to bind, directly or indirectly, to promoter DNA, to recruit RNA polymerase, or to favor elongation of a newly synthetized RNA molecule.

The nuclear membrane in eukaryotes allows further regulation of transcription factors by the duration of their presence in the nucleus which is regulated by reversible changes in their structure and by binding of other proteins. Environmental stimuli or endocrine signals may cause modification of regulatory proteins eliciting cascades of intracellular signals, which result in regulation of gene expression.

More recently it has become apparent that there is a huge influence of non-DNA-sequence specific effects on translation. These effects are referred to as epigenetic and involve the higher order structure of DNA, non-sequence specific DNA binding proteins and chemical modification of DNA. In general epigenetic effects alter the accessibility of DNA to proteins and so modulate transcription.

DNA methylation is a widespread mechanism for epigenetic influence on gene expression and is seen in bacteria and eukaryotes and has roles in heritable transcription silencing and transcription regulation. In eukaryotes the structure of chromatin, controlled by the histone code, regulates access to DNA with significant impacts on the expression of genes in euchromatin and heterochromatin areas.

Post-transcriptional Regulation

In eukaryotes, where export of RNA is required before translation is possible, nuclear export is thought to provide additional control over gene expression. All transport in and out of the nucleus is via the nuclear pore and transport is controlled by a wide range of importin and exportin proteins.

Expression of a gene coding for a protein is only possible if the messenger RNA carrying the code survives long enough to be translated. In a typical cell an RNA molecule is only stable if specifically protected from degradation. RNA degradation has particular importance in regulation of expression in eukaryotic cells where mRNA has to travel significant distances before being translated. In eukaryotes RNA is stabilised by certain post-transcriptional modifications, particularly the 5' cap and poly-adenylated tail.

Intentional degradation of mRNA is used not just as a defence mechanism from foreign RNA (normally from viruses) but also as a route of mRNA *destabilisation*. If an mRNA molecule has a complementary sequence to a small interfering RNA then it is targeted for destruction via the RNA interference pathway.

Translational Regulation

Direct regulation of translation is less prevalent than control of transcription or mRNA stability but is occasionally used. Inhibition of protein translation is a major target for toxins and antibiotics in order to kill a cell by overriding its normal gene expression control. Protein synthesis inhibitors include the antibiotic neomycin and the toxin ricin.

Protein Degradation

Once protein synthesis is complete the level of expression of that protein can be reduced by protein degradation. There are major protein degradation pathways in all prokaryotes and eukaryotes of which the proteasome is a common component. An unneeded or damaged protein is often labelled for degradation by addition of ubiquitin.

Expression System

An expression system is a system specifically designed for the production of a gene product of choice. This is normally a protein although may also be RNA, such as tRNA or a ribozyme. An expression system consists of a gene, normally encoded by DNA, and the molecular machinery required to transcribe the DNA into mRNA and translate the mRNA into protein using the reagents provided. In the broadest sense this includes every living cell but the term is more normally used to refer to expression as a laboratory tool. An expression system is therefore often artificial in some manner. Expression systems are, however, a fundamentally natural process. Viruses are an excellent example where they replicate by using the host cell as an expression system for the viral proteins and genome.

In Nature

In addition to these biological tools, certain naturally observed configurations of DNA (genes, promoters, enhancers, repressors) and the associated machinery itself are referred to as an expression system. This term is normally used in the case where a gene or set of genes is switched on under well defined conditions. For example the simple repressor 'switch' expression system in Lambda phage and the lac operator system in bacteria. Several natural expression systems are directly used or modified and used for artificial expression systems such as the Tet-on and Tet-off expression system.

Gene Networks and Expression

Genes have sometimes been regarded as nodes in a network, with inputs being proteins such as transcription factors, and outputs being the level of gene expression. The node itself performs a function, and the operation of these functions have been interpreted as performing a kind of information processing within cell and determine cellular behaviour.

Gene networks can also be constructed without formulating an explicit causal model. This is often the case when assembling networks from large expression data sets. Co-variation and correlation of expression is computed across a large sample of cases and measurements (often transcriptome or proteome data). The source of variation can be either experimental or natural (observational). There are several ways to construct gene expression networks, but one common approach is to compute a matrix of all pair-wise correlations of expression across conditions, time points, or individuals and convert the matrix (after thresholding at some cut-off value) into a graphical representation in which nodes represent genes, transcripts, or proteins and edges connecting these nodes represent the strength of association.

Genetic Code

The genetic code is the set of rules by which information encoded in genetic material (DNA or mRNA sequences) is translated into proteins (amino acid sequences) by living cells. The code defines a mapping between tri-nucleotide sequences, called codons, and amino acids. With some exceptions, a triplet codon in a nucleic acid sequence specifies a single amino acid. Because the vast majority of genes are encoded with exactly the same code , this particular code is often referred to as the canonical or standard genetic code, or simply *the* genetic code, though in fact there are many variant codes. For example, protein synthesis in human mitochondria relies on a genetic code that differs from the standard genetic code.

Not all genetic information is stored using the genetic code. All organisms' DNA contains regulatory sequences, intergenic segments, and chromosomal structural areas that can contribute greatly to phenotype. Those elements operate under sets of rules that are distinct from the codon-to-amino acid paradigm underlying the genetic code.

After the structure of DNA was deciphered by James Watson, Thomas W. Donnellan, Francis Crick, Maurice Wilkins and Rosalind Franklin, serious efforts to understand the nature of the encoding of proteins began. George Gamow postulated that a three-letter code must be employed to encode the 20 standard amino acids used by living cells to encode proteins, because 3 is the smallest integer *n* such that 4^n is at least 20.

The fact that codons consist of three DNA bases was first demonstrated in the Crick, Brenner et al. experiment. The first elucidation of a codon was done by Marshall Nirenberg and Heinrich J. Matthaei in 1961 at the National Institutes of Health. They used a cell-free system to translate a poly-uracil RNA sequence (i.e., UUUUU...) and discovered that the polypeptide that they had synthesized consisted of only the amino acid phenylalanine. They thereby deduced that the codon UUU specified the amino acid phenylalanine. This was followed by experiments in the laboratory of Severo Ochoa demonstrating that the poly-adenine RNA sequence (AAAAA...) coded for the polypeptide, poly-lysine. and the poly-cytosine RNA sequence (CCCCC...) coded for the polypeptide, poly-proline. Therefore the codon AAA specified the amino acid lysine, and the codon CCC specified the amino acid proline. Using different copolymers most of the remaining codons were then determined. Extending this work, Nirenberg and Philip Leder revealed the triplet nature of the genetic code and allowed the codons of the standard genetic code to be deciphered. In these experiments various combinations of mRNA were passed through a filter which contained ribosomes, the components of cells that translate RNA into protein. Unique triplets promoted the binding of specific tRNAs to the ribosome. Leder and Nirenberg were able to determine the sequences of 54 out of 64 codons in their experiments.

Subsequent work by Har Gobind Khorana identified the rest of the genetic code. Shortly thereafter, Robert W. Holley determined the structure of transfer RNA (tRNA), the adapter molecule that facilitates the process of translating RNA into protein. This work was based upon earlier studies by Severo

Ochoa, who received the Nobel prize in 1959 for his work on the enzymology of RNA synthesis. In 1968, Khorana, Holley and Nirenberg received the Nobel Prize in Physiology or Medicine for their work.

Transfer of Information via the Genetic Code

The genome of an organism is inscribed in DNA, or in the case of some viruses, RNA. The portion of the genome that codes for a protein or an RNA is referred to as a gene. Those genes that code for proteins are composed of tri-nucleotide units called codons, each coding for a single amino acid. Each nucleotide sub-unit consists of a phosphate, deoxyribose sugar and one of the 4 nitrogenous nucleobases. The purine bases adenine (*A*) and guanine (*G*) are larger and consist of two aromatic rings. The pyrimidine bases cytosine (C) and thymine (*T*) are smaller and consist of only one aromatic ring. In the double-helix configuration, two strands of DNA are joined to each other by hydrogen bonds in an arrangement known as base pairing. These bonds almost always form between an adenine base on one strand and a thymine on the other strand and between a cytosine base on one strand and a guanine base on the other. This means that the number of *A* and *T* residues will be the same in a given double helix, as will the number of *G* and *C* residues. :102–117 In RNA, thymine (*T*) is replaced by uracil (*U*), and the deoxyribose is substituted by ribose.

Each protein-coding gene is transcribed into a template molecule of the related polymer RNA, known as messenger RNA or mRNA. This, in turn, is translated on the ribosome into an amino acid chain or polypeptide. The process of translation requires transfer RNAs specific for individual amino acids with the amino acids covalently attached to them, guanosine triphosphate as an energy source, and a number of translation factors. tRNAs have anticodons complementary to the codons in mRNA and can be 'charged' covalently with amino acids at their 3′ terminal CCA ends.

Individual tRNAs are charged with specific amino acids by enzymes known as aminoacyl tRNA synthetases, which have high specificity for both their cognate amino acids and tRNAs. The high specificity of these enzymes is a major reason why the fidelity of protein translation is maintained.

There are $4^3 = 64$ different codon combinations possible with a triplet codon of three nucleotides; all 64 codons are assigned for either amino acids or stop signals during translation. If, for example, an RNA sequence, UUUAAACCC is considered and the reading frame starts with the first *U* (by convention, 5' to 3'), there are three codons, namely, UUU, AAA and CCC, each of which specifies one amino acid. This RNA sequence will be translated into an amino acid sequence, three amino acids long. : A comparison may be made with computer science, where the codon is similar to a word, which is the standard 'chunk' for handling data (like one amino acid of a protein), and a nucleotide is similar to a bit, in that it is the smallest unit.

Sequence Reading Frame

A codon is defined by the initial nucleotide from which translation starts. For example, the string GGGAAACCC, if read from the first position, contains the codons GGG, AAA and CCC; and, if read from the second position, it contains the codons GGA and AAC; if read starting from the third position, GAA and ACC. Every sequence can thus be read in three reading frames, each of which will produce a different amino acid sequence (in the given example, Gly-Lys-Pro, Gly-Asn, or Glu-Thr, respectively). With double-stranded DNA there are six possible reading frames, three in the forward orientation on one strand and three reverse on the opposite strand: 330 The actual frame in which a protein sequence is translated is defined by a start codon, usually the first AUG codon in the mRNA sequence.

Start/Stop Codons

Translation starts with a chain initiation codon (start codon). Unlike stop codons, the codon alone is not sufficient to begin the process. Nearby sequences (such as the Shine-Dalgarno sequence in *E. coli*) and initiation factors are also required to start translation. The most common start codon is AUG which is read as methionine or, in bacteria, as formylmethionine. Alternative start codons (depending on the organism), include 'GUG' or 'UUG', which normally code for valine or leucine, respectively. However, when used as a start codon, these alternative start codons are translated as methionine or formylmethionine.

The three stop codons have been given names: UAG is *amber*, UGA is *opal* (sometimes also called *umber*), and UAA is *ochre*. 'Amber' was named by discoverers Richard Epstein and Charles Steinberg after their friend Harris Bernstein, whose last name means 'amber' in German. The other two stop codons were named 'ochre' and 'opal' in order to keep the 'colour names'" theme. Stop codons are also called 'termination' or 'nonsense' codons and they signal release of the nascent polypeptide from the ribosome due to binding of release factors in the absence of cognate tRNAs with anticodons complementary to these stop signals.

During the process of DNA replication, errors occasionally occur in the polymerization of the second strand. These errors, called mutations, can have an impact on the phenotype of an organism, especially if they occur within the protein coding sequence of a gene. Error rates are usually very low–1 error in every 10-100 million bases–due to the 'proofreading' ability of DNA polymerases.

Missense mutations and nonsense mutations are examples of point mutations, which can cause genetic diseases such as sickle-cell disease and thalassemia respectively. Clinically important missense mutations generally change the properties of the coded amino acid residue between being basic, acidic polar or non-polar, whereas nonsense mutations result in a stop codon.

Mutations that disrupt the reading frame sequence by indels (insertions or deletions) of a non-multiple of 3 nucleotide bases are known as frameshift mutations. These mutations usually result in a completely different translation from the original, and are also very likely to cause a stop codon to be read, which truncates the creation of the protein. These mutations may impair the function of the resulting protein, and are thus rare in *in vivo* protein-coding sequences. One reason inheritance of frameshift mutations is rare is that if the protein being translated is essential for growth under the selective pressures the organism faces, absence of a functional protein may cause death before the organism is viable. Frameshift mutations may result in severe genetic diseases such as Tay-Sachs disease.

Although most mutations that change protein sequences are harmful or neutral, some mutations have a positive effect on an organism. These mutations may enable the mutant organism to withstand particular environmental stresses better than wild-type organisms, or reproduce more quickly. In these cases a mutation will tend to become more common in a population through natural selection. Viruses that use RNA as their genetic material have rapid mutation rates, which can be an advantage since these viruses will evolve constantly and rapidly, and thus evade the defensive responses of e.g. the human immune system. In large populations of asexually reproducing organisms, for example, E. coli, multiple beneficial mutations may co-occur, causing competition among them, this phenomenon is called clonal interference.

Degeneracy of the Genetic Code

The genetic code has redundancy but no ambiguity (see the codon tables above for the full correlation). For example, although codons GAA and GAG both specify glutamic acid (redundancy), neither of them specifies any other amino acid (no ambiguity). The codons encoding one amino acid may differ in any of their three positions. For example the amino acid glutamic acid is specified by GAA and GAG codons (difference in the third position), the amino acid leucine is specified by UUA, UUG, CUU, CUC, CUA, CUG codons (difference in the first or third position), while the amino acid serine is specified by UCA, UCG, UCC, UCU, AGU, AGC (difference in the first, second or third position).

A position of a codon is said to be a fourfold degenerate site if any nucleotide at this position specifies the same amino acid. For example, the third position of the glycine codons (GGA, GGG, GGC, GGU) is a four-fold degenerate site, because all nucleotide substitutions at this site are synonymous; i.e., they do not change the amino acid. Only the third positions of some codons may be four-fold degenerate. A position of a codon is said to be a two-fold degenerate site if only two of four possible nucleotides at this position specify the same amino acid. For example, the third position of the glutamic acid codons (GAA, GAG) is a two-fold degenerate site. In two-fold degenerate sites, the equivalent nucleotides are always either two purines (A/G) or two pyrimidines (C/U), so only transversional substitutions (purine to pyrimidine or pyrimidine to purine) in two-fold degenerate sites are nonsynonymous. A position of a codon is said to be a non-degenerate site if any mutation at this position results in amino acid substitution. There is only one three-fold degenerate site where changing to three of the four nucleotides may have no effect on the amino acid (depending on what it is changed to), while changing to the fourth possible nucleotide always results in an amino acid substitution. This is the third position of an isoleucine codon: AUU, AUC, or AUA all encode isoleucine, but AUG encodes methionine. In computation this position is often treated as a two-fold degenerate site.

There are three amino acids encoded by six different codons: serine, leucine, and arginine. Only two amino acids are specified by a single codon. One of these is the amino-acid methionine, specified by the codon AUG, which also specifies the start of translation; the other is tryptophan, specified by the codon UGG. The degeneracy of the genetic code is what accounts for the existence of synonymous mutations.

Degeneracy results because there are more codons than encodable amino acids. For example, if there were two bases per codon, then only 16 amino acids could be coded for (4^2=16). Because at least 21 codes are required (20 amino acids plus stop), and the next largest number of bases is three, then 4^3 gives 64 possible codons, meaning that some degeneracy must exist.

These properties of the genetic code make it more fault-tolerant for point mutations. For example, in theory, four-fold degenerate codons can tolerate any point mutation at the third position, although codon usage bias restricts this in practice in many organisms; two-fold degenerate codons can tolerate one out of the three possible point mutations at the third position. Since transition mutations (purine to purine or pyrimidine to pyrimidine mutations) are more likely than transversion (purine to pyrimidine or vice-versa) mutations, the equivalence of purines or that of pyrimidines at two-fold degenerate sites adds a further fault-tolerance.

A practical consequence of redundancy is that some errors in the genetic code only cause a silent mutation or an error that would not affect the protein because the hydrophilicity or hydrophobicity is maintained by equivalent substitution of amino acids; for example, a codon of NUN (where N = any nucleotide) tends to code for hydrophobic amino acids. NCN yields amino acid residues that are small in size and moderate in hydropathy; NAN encodes average size hydrophilic residues. These tendencies may result from the shared ancestry of the aminoacyl tRNA synthetases related to these codons.

Even so, single point mutations can still cause dysfunctional proteins. For example, a mutated haemoglobin gene causes sickle-cell disease. In the mutant haemoglobin a hydrophilic glutamate (Glu) is substituted by the hydrophobic valine (Val), that is, GAA or GAG becomes GUA or GUG. The substitution of glutamate by valine reduces the solubility of ß-globin which causes hemoglobin to form linear polymers linked by the hydrophobic interaction between the valine groups causing sickle-cell deformation of erythrocytes. Sickle-cell disease is generally not caused by a *de novo* mutation. Rather it is selected for in malarial regions (in a way similar to thalassemia), as heterozygous people have some resistance to the malarial *Plasmodium* parasite (heterozygote advantage).

These variable codes for amino acids are allowed because of modified bases in the first base of the anticodon of the tRNA, and the base-pair formed is called a wobble base pair. The modified bases include inosine and the Non-Watson-Crick U-G basepair.

Variations to the Standard Genetic Code

While slight variations on the standard code had been predicted earlier, none were discovered until 1979, when researchers studying human mitochondrial genes discovered they used an alternative code. Many slight variants have been discovered since, including various alternative mitochondrial codes, as well as small variants such as *Mycoplasma* translating the codon UGA as tryptophan and *Candida* species translating CUG as a serine rather than a leucine. In bacteria and archaea, GUG and UUG are common start codons. However, in rare cases, certain specific proteins may use alternative initiation (start) codons not normally used by that species.

In certain proteins, non-standard amino acids are substituted for standard stop codons, depending upon associated signal sequences in the messenger RNA: UGA can code for selenocysteine and UAG can code for pyrrolysine as discussed in the relevant articles. Selenocysteine is now viewed as the 21st amino acid, and pyrrolysine is viewed as the 22nd.

Notwithstanding these differences, all known codes have strong similarities to each other, and the coding mechanism is the same for all organisms: three-base codons, tRNA, ribosomes, reading the code in the same direction and translating the code three letters at a time into sequences of amino acids.

Expanded Genetic Code

Since 2001, 40 non-natural amino acids have been added into protein by creating a unique codon (recoding) and a corresponding transfer-RNA:aminoacyl — tRNA-synthetase pair to encode it with diverse physicochemical and biological properties in order to be used as a tool to exploring protein structure and function or to create novel or enhanced proteins.

Theories on the Origin of the Genetic Code

Despite the minor variations that exist, the genetic code used by all known forms of life is nearly universal. However, there are a huge number of possible genetic codes. If amino acids are randomly associated with triplet codons, there will be 1.5×10^{84} possible genetic codes. The question arises: why this code? How did it originate?

Phylogenetic analysis of transfer RNA suggests that tRNA molecules evolved before the present set of aminoacyl-tRNA synthetases.

Theoretically the genetic code could be completely random (a 'frozen accident'), completely non-random (optimal) or a combination of random and non-random. There are sufficient data to refute the first possibility. For a start, a quick view on the table of the genetic code already shows a clustering of amino acid assignments. Furthermore, amino acids that share the same biosynthetic pathway tend to have the same first base in their codons, and amino acids with similar physical properties tend to have similar codons.

There are four themes running through the many theories that seek to explain the evolution of the genetic code (and hence the origin of these patterns):

1. Chemical principles govern specific RNA interaction with amino acids. Aptamer experiments showed that some amino acids have a selective chemical affinity for the base triplets that code for them. Recent experiments show that of the 8 amino acids tested, 6 show some RNA triplet-amino acid association. This has been called the stereochemical code. The stereochemical code could have created an ancient core of assignments. The current complex translation mechanism involving tRNA and associated enzymes may be a later development, and that originally, protein sequences were directly templated on base sequences.
2. Biosynthetic expansion. The standard modern genetic code grew from a simpler earlier code through a process of 'biosynthetic expansion'. Here the idea is that primordial life 'discovered' new amino acids (e.g., as by-products of metabolism) and later back-incorporated some of these into the machinery of genetic coding. Although much circumstantial evidence has been found to suggest that fewer different amino acids were used in the past than today, precise and detailed hypotheses about exactly which amino acids entered the code in exactly what order have proved far more controversial.
3. Natural selection has led to codon assignments of the genetic code that minimize the effects of mutations. A recent hypothesis suggests that the triplet code was derived from codes that used longer than triplet codons. Longer than triplet decoding has higher degree of codon redundancy and is more error resistant than the triplet decoding. This feature could allow accurate decoding in the absence of highly complex translational machinery such as the ribosome.
4. Information channels: Information-theoretic approaches see the genetic code as an error-prone information channel. The inherent noise (i.e. errors) in the channel

poses the organism with a fundamental question: how to construct a genetic code that can withstand the impact of noise while accurately and efficiently translating information? These 'rate-distortion' models suggest that the genetic code originated as a result of the interplay of the three conflicting evolutionary forces: the needs for diverse amino-acids, for error-tolerance and for minimal cost of resources. The code emerges at a coding transition when the mapping of codons to amino-acids becomes nonrandom. The emergence of the code is governed by the topology defined by the probable errors and is related to the map colouring problem.

Mendelian Inheritance

Mendelian inheritance (or Mendelian genetics or Mendelism) is a set of primary tenets relating to the transmission of hereditary characteristics from parent organisms to their offspring; it underlies much of genetics. They were initially derived from the work of Gregor Mendel published in 1865 and 1866 which was 're-discovered' in 1900, and were initially very controversial. When they were integrated with the chromosome theory of inheritance by Thomas Hunt Morgan in 1915, they became the core of classical genetics.

The laws of inheritance were derived by Gregor Mendel, a 19th century Austrian Priest/monk conducting hybridization experiments in garden peas (*Pisum sativum*). Between 1856 and 1863, he cultivated and tested some 29,000 pea plants. From these experiments he deduced two generalizations which later became known as *Mendel's Principles of Heredity* or *Mendelian inheritance*. He described these principles in a two part paper, *Experiments on Plant Hybridization* that he read to the Natural History Society of Brno on February 8 and March 8, 1865, and which was published in 1866.

Mendel's conclusions were largely ignored. Although they were not completely unknown to biologists of the time, they were not seen as generally applicable, even by Mendel himself, who thought they only applied to certain categories of species or traits. A major block to understanding their significance was the importance attached by 19th century biologists to the apparent blending of inherited traits in the overall appearance of the progeny, now known to be due to multigene interactions, in contrast to the organ-specific binary characters studied by Mendel. In 1900, however, his work was 're-discovered' by three European scientists, Hugo de Vries, Carl Correns, and Erich von Tschermak. The exact nature of the 're-discovery' has been somewhat debated: De Vries published first on the subject, mentioning Mendel in a footnote, while Correns pointed out Mendel's priority after having read De Vries's paper and realizing that he himself did not have priority. De Vries may not have acknowledged truthfully how much of his knowledge of the laws came from his own work, or came only after reading Mendel's paper. Later scholars have accused Von Tschermak of not truly understanding the results at all.

Regardless, the 're-discovery' made Mendelism an important but controversial theory. Its most vigorous promoter in Europe was William Bateson, who coined the term 'genetics', 'gene', and 'allele' to describe many of its tenets. The model of heredity was highly contested by other biologists because it implied that heredity was discontinuous, in opposition to the apparently continuous variation observable for many traits. Many biologists also dismissed the theory because they were not sure it would apply to all species, and there seemed to be very few true Mendelian characters in nature. However later work by biologists and statisticians such as R.A. Fisher showed that if multiple Mendelian factors were involved in the expression of an individual trait, they could produce the diverse results observed. Thomas Hunt Morgan and his assistants later integrated the theoretical model of Mendel with the chromosome theory of inheritance, in which the chromosomes of cells were thought to hold the actual hereditary material, and create what is now known as classical genetics, which was extremely successful and cemented Mendel's place in history.

Mendel's findings allowed other scientists to predict the expression of traits on the basis of mathematical probabilities. A large contribution to Mendel's success can be traced to his decision to start his crosses only with plants he demonstrated were true-breeding. He also only measured absolute (binary) characteristics, such as color, shape, and position of the offspring, rather than quantitative characteristics. He expressed his results numerically and subjected them to statistical analysis. His method of data analysis and his large sample size gave credibility to his data. He also had the foresight to follow several successive generations (*f2*, *f3*) of his pea plants and record their variations. Finally, he performed 'test crosses' (back-crossing descendants of the initial hybridization to the initial true-breeding lines) to reveal the presence and proportion of recessive characters. Without his hard work and careful attention to procedure and detail, Mendel's work could not have had the impact it made on the world of genetics.

Mendel's Laws

Mendel discovered that by crossing white flower and purple flower plants, the result was not a blend. Rather than being a mix of the two, the offspring was purple flowered. He then conceived the idea of heredity units, which he called 'factors', one of which is a recessive characteristic and the other dominant. Mendel said that factors, later called genes, normally occur in pairs in ordinary body cells, yet segregate during the formation of sex cells. Each member of the pair becomes part of the separate sex cell. The dominant gene, such as the purple flower in Mendel's plants, will hide the recessive gene, the white flower. After Mendel self-fertilized the *F1* generation and obtained the 3:1 ratio, he correctly theorized that genes can be paired in three different ways for each trait: *AA*, *aa*, and *Aa*. The capital '*A*' represents the dominant factor and lowercase '*a*' represents the recessive. (The last combination listed above, *Aa*, will occur roughly twice as often as each of the other two, as it can be made in two different ways, *Aa* or *aA*.)

Mendel stated that each individual has two factors for each trait, one from each parent. The two factors may or may not contain the same information. If the two factors are identical, the individual is called homozygous for the trait. If the two factors have different information, the individual is called heterozygous. The alternative forms of a factor are called alleles. The genotype of an individual is made up of the many alleles it possesses. An individual's physical appearance, or phenotype, is determined by its alleles as well as by its environment. An individual possesses two alleles for each trait; one allele is given by the female parent and the other by the male parent. They are passed on when an individual matures and produces gametes: egg and sperm. When gametes form, the paired alleles separate randomly so that each gamete receives a copy of one of the two alleles. The presence of an allele doesn't promise that the trait will be expressed in the individual that possesses it. In heterozygous individuals the only allele that is expressed is the dominant. The recessive allele is present but its expression is hidden.

Mendel summarized his findings in two laws; the Law of Segregation and the Law of Independent Assortment.

Law of Segregation (The 'First Law')

The Law of Segregation states that when any individual produces gametes, the copies of a gene separate so that each gamete receives only one copy. A gamete will receive one allele or the other. The direct proof of this was later found following the observation of meiosis by two independent scientists, the German botanist, Oscar Hertwig in 1876, and the Belgian zoologist, Edouard Van Beneden in 1883. In meiosis the paternal and maternal chromosomes get separated and the alleles with the traits of a character are segregated into two different gametes.

Law of Independent Assortment (The 'Second Law')

The Law of Independent Assortment, also known as 'Inheritance Law', states that alleles of different genes assort independently of one another during gamete formation. While Mendel's experiments with mixing one trait always resulted in a 3:1 ratio between dominant and recessive phenotypes, his experiments with mixing two traits (dihybrid cross) showed 9:3:3:1 ratios . But the 9:3:3:1 shows that each of the two genes are independently inherited with a 3:1 phenotypic ratio. Mendel concluded that different traits are inherited independently of each other, so that there is no relation, for example, between a cat's colour and tail length. This is actually only true for genes that are not linked to each other.

Independent assortment occurs during meiosis I in eukaryotic organisms, specifically anaphase I of *meiosis,* to produce a gamete with a mixture of the organism's maternal and paternal chromosomes. Along with chromosomal crossover, this process aids in increasing genetic diversity by producing novel genetic combinations.

Of the 46 chromosomes in a normal diploid human cell, half are maternally-derived (from the mother's egg) and half are paternally-derived (from the father's sperm). This occurs as sexual reproduction involves the fusion of two haploid gametes (the egg and sperm) to produce a new organism having the full complement of chromosomes. During gametogenesis—the production of new gametes by an adult– the normal complement of 46 chromosomes needs to be halved to 23 to ensure that the resulting haploid gamete can join with another gamete to produce a diploid organism. An error in the number of chromosomes, such as those caused by a diploid gamete joining with a haploid gamete, is termed aneuploidy.

In independent assortment the chromosomes that end up in a newly-formed gamete are randomly sorted from all possible combinations of maternal and paternal chromosomes. Because gametes end up with a random mix instead of a pre-defined 'set' from either parent, gametes are therefore considered assorted independently. As such, the gamete can end up with any combination of paternal or maternal chromosomes. Any of the possible combinations of gametes formed from maternal and paternal chromosomes will occur with equal frequency. For human gametes, with 23 pairs of chromosomes, the number of possibilities is 2^{23} or 8,388,608 possible combinations. The gametes will normally end up with 23 chromosomes, but the origin of any particular one will be randomly selected from paternal or maternal chromosomes. This contributes to the genetic variability of progeny.

The reason for these laws is found in the nature of the cell nucleus. It is made up of several chromosomes carrying the genetic traits. In a normal cell, each of these chromosomes has two parts, the chromatids. A reproductive cell, which is created in a process called meiosis, usually contains only one of those chromatids of each chromosome. By merging two of these cells (usually one male and one female), the full set is restored and the genes are mixed. The resulting cell becomes a new embryo. The fact that this new life has half the genes of each parent (23 from mother, 23 from father for total of 46 in the case of humans) is one reason for the Mendelian laws. The second most important reason is the varying dominance of different genes, causing some traits to appear unevenly instead of averaging out (whereby dominant doesn't mean more likely to reproduce—recessive genes can become the most common, too).

There are several advantages of this method (sexual reproduction) over reproduction without genetic exchange.

Instead of nearly identical copies of an organism, a broad range of offspring develops, allowing more different abilities and evolutionary strategies.

There are usually some errors in every cell nucleus. Copying the genes usually adds more of them. By distributing them randomly over different chromosomes and mixing the genes, such errors will be distributed unevenly over the different children. Some of them will therefore have only very few such problems. This helps reduce problems with copying errors somewhat.

Genes can spread faster from one part of a population to another. This is for instance useful if there's a temporary isolation of two groups. New genes developing in each of the populations don't get reduced to half when one side replaces the other, they mix and form a population with the advantages of both sides.

Sometimes, a mutation (e. g. sickle cell anaemia) can have positive side effects (in this case malaria resistance). The mechanism behind the Mendelian laws can make it possible for some offspring to carry the advantages without the disadvantages until further mutations solve the problems.

A Mendelian trait is one that is controlled by a single locus and shows a simple Mendelian inheritance pattern. In such cases, a mutation in a single gene can cause a disease that is inherited according to Mendel's laws. Examples include sickle-cell anaemia, Tay-Sachs disease, cystic fibrosis and xeroderma pigmentosa. A disease controlled by a single gene contrasts with a multi-factorial disease, like arthritis, which is affected by several loci (and the environment) as well as those diseases inherited in a non-Mendelian fashion. The Mendelian Inheritance in Man database is a catalog of, among other things, genes in which Mendelian traits cause disease.

Deoxyribonucleic Acid

Deoxyribonucleic acid (DNA) is a nucleic acid that contains the genetic instructions used in the development and functioning of all known living organisms with the exception of some viruses. The main role of DNA molecules is the long-term storage of information. DNA is often compared to a set of blueprints, like a recipe or a code, since it contains the instructions needed to construct other components of cells, such as proteins and RNA molecules. The DNA segments that carry this genetic information are called genes, but other DNA sequences have structural purposes, or are involved in regulating the use of this genetic information.

DNA consists of two long polymers of simple units called nucleotides, with backbones made of sugars and phosphate groups joined by ester bonds. These two strands run in opposite directions to each other and are therefore anti-parallel. Attached to each sugar is one of four types of molecules called bases. It is the sequence of these four bases along the backbone that encodes information. This information is read using the genetic code, which specifies the sequence of the amino acids within proteins. The code is read by copying stretches of DNA into the related nucleic acid RNA, in a process called transcription.

Within cells, DNA is organized into long structures called chromosomes. These chromosomes are duplicated before cells divide, in a process called DNA replication. Eukaryotic organisms (animals, plants, fungi, and protists) store most of their DNA inside the cell nucleus and some of their DNA in organelles, such as mitochondria or chloroplasts. In contrast, prokaryotes (bacteria and archaea) store their DNA only in the cytoplasm. Within the chromosomes, chromatin proteins such as histones compact and organize DNA. These compact structures guide the interactions between DNA and other proteins, helping control which parts of the DNA are transcribed.

DNA is a long polymer made from repeating units called nucleotides. As first discovered by James D. Watson and Francis Crick, the structure of DNA of all species comprises two helical chains each coiled round the same access, and each with a pitch of 34 Ångströms (3.4 nanometres) and a radius of 10 Ångströms (1.0 nanometres). According to another study, when measured in a particular solution, the DNA chain measured 22 to 26 Ångströms wide (2.2 to 2.6 nanometres), and one nucleotide unit measured 3.3 Å (0.33 nm) long. Although each individual repeating unit is very small, DNA polymers can be very large molecules containing millions of nucleotides. For instance, the largest human chromosome, chromosome number 1, is approximately 220 million base pairs long.

In living organisms, DNA does not usually exist as a single molecule, but instead as a pair of molecules that are held tightly together. These two long strands entwine like vines, in the shape of a double helix. The nucleotide repeats contain both the segment of the backbone of the molecule, which holds the chain together, and a base, which interacts with the other DNA strand in the helix. A base linked to a sugar is called a nucleoside and a base linked to a sugar and one or more phosphate groups is called a nucleotide. If multiple nucleotides are linked together, as in DNA, this polymer is called a polynucleotide.

The backbone of the DNA strand is made from alternating phosphate and sugar residues. The sugar in DNA is 2-deoxyribose, which is a pentose (five-carbon) sugar. The sugars are joined together by phosphate groups that form phosphodiester bonds between the third and fifth carbon atoms of adjacent sugar rings. These asymmetric bonds mean a strand of DNA has a direction. In a double helix the direction of the nucleotides in one strand is opposite to their direction in the other strand: the strands are *antiparallel*. The asymmetric ends of DNA strands are called the 5' (*five prime*) and 3' (*three prime*) ends, with the 5' end having a terminal phosphate group and the 3' end a terminal hydroxyl group. One major difference between DNA and RNA is the sugar, with the 2-deoxyribose in DNA being replaced by the alternative pentose sugar ribose in RNA.

The DNA double helix is stabilized by hydrogen bonds between the bases attached to the two strands. The four bases found in DNA are adenine (abbreviated A), cytosine (C), guanine (G) and thymine (T). These four bases are attached to the sugar/phosphate to form the complete nucleotide, as shown for adenosine monophosphate.

These bases are classified into two types; adenine and guanine are fused five- and six-membered heterocyclic compounds called purines, while cytosine and thymine are six-membered rings called pyrimidines. A fifth pyrimidine base, called uracil (U), usually takes the place of thymine in RNA and differs from thymine by lacking a methyl group on its ring. Uracil is not usually found in DNA, occurring only as a breakdown product of cytosine. In addition to RNA and DNA, a large number of artificial nucleic acid analogues have also been created to study the proprieties of nucleic acids, or for use in biotechnology.

Twin helical strands form the DNA backbone. Another double helix may be found by tracing the spaces, or grooves, between the strands. These voids are adjacent to the base pairs and may provide a binding site. As the strands are not directly opposite each other, the grooves are unequally sized. One groove, the major groove, is 22 Å wide and the other, the minor groove, is 12 Å wide. The narrowness of the minor groove means that the edges of the bases are more accessible in the major groove. As a result, proteins like transcription factors that can bind to specific sequences in double-stranded DNA usually make contacts to the sides of the bases exposed in the major groove. This situation varies in unusual conformations of DNA within the cell *(see below)*, but the major and minor grooves are always named to reflect the differences in size that would be seen if the DNA is twisted back into the ordinary B form.

Base Pairing

Each type of base on one strand forms a bond with just one type of base on the other strand. This is called complementary base pairing. Here, purines form hydrogen bonds to pyrimidines, with *A* bonding only to *T*, and *C* bonding only to *G*. This arrangement of two nucleotides binding together across the double helix is called a base pair. As hydrogen bonds are not covalent, they can be broken and rejoined relatively easily. The two strands of DNA in a double helix can therefore be pulled apart like a zipper, either by a mechanical force or high temperature. As a result of this complementarity, all the information in the double-stranded sequence of a DNA helix is duplicated on each strand, which is vital in DNA replication. Indeed, this reversible and specific interaction between complementary base pairs is critical for all the functions of DNA in living organisms.

The two types of base pairs form different numbers of hydrogen bonds, *AT* forming two hydrogen bonds, and *GC* forming three hydrogen bonds. DNA with high *GC*-content is more stable than DNA with low *GC*-content, but contrary to popular belief, this is not due to the extra hydrogen bond of a *GC* base pair but rather the contribution of stacking interactions (hydrogen bonding merely provides specificity of the pairing, not stability). As a result, it is both the percentage of *GC* base pairs and the overall length of a DNA double helix that determine the strength of the association between the two strands of DNA. Long DNA helices with a high *GC* content have stronger-interacting strands, while short helices with high AT content have weaker-interacting strands. In biology, parts of the DNA double helix that need to separate easily, such as the TATAAT Pribnow box in some promoters, tend to have a high *AT* content, making the strands easier to pull apart. In the laboratory, the strength of this interaction can be measured by finding the temperature required to break the hydrogen bonds, their melting temperature (also called T_m value). When all the base pairs in a DNA double helix melt, the strands separate and exist in solution as two entirely independent molecules. These single-stranded DNA molecules (*ssDNA*) have no single common shape, but some conformations are more stable than others.

A DNA sequence is called 'sense' if its sequence is the same as that of a messenger RNA copy that is translated into protein. The sequence on the opposite strand is called the 'antisense' sequence. Both sense and antisense sequences can exist on different parts of the same strand of DNA (i.e. both strands contain both sense and antisense sequences). In both prokaryotes and eukaryotes, antisense RNA sequences are produced, but the functions of these RNAs are not entirely clear. One proposal is that antisense RNAs are involved in regulating gene expression through RNA-RNA base pairing.

A few DNA sequences in prokaryotes and eukaryotes, and more in plasmids and viruses, blur the distinction between sense and antisense strands by having overlapping genes. In these cases, some DNA sequences do double duty, encoding one protein when read along one strand, and a second protein when read in the opposite direction along the other strand. In bacteria, this overlap may be involved in the regulation of gene transcription, while in viruses, overlapping genes increase the amount of information that can be encoded within the small viral genome.

Supercoiling

DNA can be twisted like a rope in a process called DNA supercoiling. With DNA in its 'relaxed'" state, a strand usually circles the axis of the double helix once every 10.4 base pairs, but if the DNA is twisted the strands become more tightly or more loosely wound. If the DNA is twisted in the direction of the helix, this is positive supercoiling, and the bases are held more tightly together. If they are twisted in the opposite direction, this is negative supercoiling, and the bases come apart more easily. In nature, most DNA has slight negative supercoiling that is introduced by enzymes called topoisomerases. These enzymes are also needed to relieve the twisting stresses introduced into DNA strands during processes such as transcription and DNA replication.

DNA exists in many possible conformations that include A-DNA, B-DNA, and Z-DNA forms, although, only B-DNA and Z-DNA have been directly observed in functional organisms. The conformation that DNA adopts depends on the hydration level, DNA sequence, the amount and direction of supercoiling, chemical modifications of the bases, the type and concentration of metal ions, as well as the presence of polyamines in solution.

The first published reports of A-DNA X-ray diffraction patterns—and also B-DNA used analyses based on Patterson transforms that provided only a limited amount of structural information for oriented fibers of DNA. An alternate analysis was then proposed by Wilkins *et al.*, in 1953, for the *in vivo* B-DNA X-ray diffraction/scattering patterns of highly hydrated DNA fibers in terms of squares of Bessel functions. In the same journal, James D. Watson and Francis Crick presented their molecular modeling analysis of the DNA X-ray diffraction patterns to suggest that the structure was a double-helix.

Although the 'B-DNA form' is most common under the conditions found in cells, it is not a well-defined conformation but a family of related DNA conformations that occur at the high hydration levels present in living cells.

Their corresponding X-ray diffraction and scattering patterns are characteristic of molecular paracrystals with a significant degree of disorder.

Compared to B-DNA, the A-DNA form is a wider right-handed spiral, with a shallow, wide minor groove and a narrower, deeper major groove. The *A* form occurs under non-physiological conditions in partially dehydrated samples of DNA, while in the cell it may be produced in hybrid pairings of DNA and RNA strands, as well as in enzyme-DNA complexes. Segments of DNA where the bases have been chemically modified by methylation may undergo a larger change in conformation and adopt the *Z* form. Here, the strands turn about the helical axis in a left-handed spiral, the opposite of the more common *B* form. These unusual structures can be recognized by specific Z-DNA binding proteins and may be involved in the regulation of transcription.

At the ends of the linear chromosomes are specialized regions of DNA called telomeres. The main function of these regions is to allow the cell to replicate chromosome ends using the enzyme telomerase, as the enzymes that normally replicate DNA cannot copy the extreme 3' ends of chromosomes. These specialized chromosome caps also help protect the DNA ends, and stop the DNA repair systems in the cell from treating them as damage to be corrected. In human cells, telomeres are usually lengths of single-stranded DNA containing several thousand repeats of a simple TTAGGG sequence.

These guanine-rich sequences may stabilize chromosome ends by forming structures of stacked sets of four-base units, rather than the usual base pairs found in other DNA molecules. Here, four guanine bases form a flat plate and these flat four-base units then stack on top of each other, to form a stable *G-quadruplex* structure. These structures are stabilized by hydrogen bonding between the edges of the bases and chelation of a metal ion in the centre of each four-base unit. Other structures can also be formed, with the central set of four bases coming from either a single strand folded around the bases, or several different parallel strands, each contributing one base to the central structure.

In addition to these stacked structures, telomeres also form large loop structures called telomere loops, or T-loops. Here, the single-stranded DNA curls around in a long circle stabilized by telomere-binding proteins. At the very end of the T-loop, the single-stranded telomere DNA is held onto a region of double-stranded DNA by the telomere strand disrupting the double-helical DNA and base pairing to one of the two strands. This triple-stranded structure is called a displacement loop or D-loop.

The expression of genes is influenced by how the DNA is packaged in chromosomes, in a structure called chromatin. Base modifications can be involved in packaging, with regions that have low or no gene expression usually containing high levels of methylation of cytosine bases. For example, cytosine methylation, produces 5-methylcytosine, which is important for X-chromosome inactivation. The average level of methylation varies between organisms — the worm *Caenorhabditis elegans* lacks cytosine methylation, while vertebrates have higher levels, with up to 1 per cent of their DNA containing 5-methylcytosine. Despite the importance of 5-methylcytosine, it can deaminate to leave a thymine base, so methylated cytosines are particularly prone to mutations. Other base modifications include adenine methylation in bacteria, the presence of 5-hydroxymethylcytosine in the brain, and the glycosylation of uracil to produce the 'J-base' in kinetoplastids.

Branched DNA

In DNA fraying occurs when non-complementary regions exist at the end of an otherwise complementary double-strand of DNA. However, branched DNA can occur if a third strand of DNA is introduced and contains adjoining regions able to hybridize with the frayed regions of the pre-existing double-strand. Although the simplest example of branched DNA involves only three strands of DNA, complexes involving additional strands and multiple branches are also possible. Branched DNA can be used in nanotechnology to construct geometric shapes, see the section on uses in technology below.

DNA can be damaged by many sorts of mutagens, which change the DNA sequence. Mutagens include oxidizing agents, alkylating agents and also high-energy electromagnetic radiation such as ultraviolet light and X-rays. The type of DNA damage produced depends on the type of mutagen. For example, UV light can damage DNA by producing thymine dimers, which are cross-links between pyrimidine bases. On the other hand, oxidants such as free radicals or hydrogen peroxide produce multiple forms of damage, including base modifications, particularly of guanosine, and double-strand breaks. A typical human cell contains about 150,000 bases that have suffered oxidative damage. Of these oxidative lesions, the most dangerous are double-strand breaks, as these are difficult to repair and can produce point mutations, insertions and deletions from the DNA sequence, as well as chromosomal translocations.

Many mutagens fit into the space between two adjacent base pairs, this is called *intercalation*. Most intercalators are aromatic and planar molecules; examples include ethidium bromide, daunomycin, and doxorubicin. In order for an intercalator to fit between base pairs, the bases must separate, distorting the DNA strands by unwinding of the double helix. This inhibits both transcription and DNA replication, causing toxicity and mutations. As a result, DNA intercalators are often carcinogens, and benzo[*a*]pyrene diol epoxide, acridines, aflatoxin and ethidium bromide are well-known examples. Nevertheless, due to their ability to inhibit DNA transcription and replication, other similar toxins are also used in chemotherapy to inhibit rapidly growing cancer cells.

Biological Functions

DNA usually occurs as linear chromosomes in eukaryotes, and circular chromosomes in prokaryotes. The set of chromosomes in a cell makes up its genome; the human genome has approximately 3 billion base pairs of DNA arranged into 46 chromosomes. The information carried by DNA is held in the sequence of pieces of DNA called genes. Transmission of genetic information in genes is achieved via complementary base pairing. For example, in transcription, when a cell uses the information in a gene, the DNA sequence is copied into a complementary RNA sequence through the attraction between the DNA and the correct RNA nucleotides. Usually, this RNA copy is then used to make a matching protein sequence in a process called translation, which depends on the same interaction between RNA nucleotides. In alternative fashion, a cell may simply copy its genetic information in a process called DNA replication. The details of these functions are covered in other articles; here we focus on the interactions between DNA and other molecules that mediate the function of the genome.

Genes and Genomes

Genomic DNA is tightly and orderly packed in the process called DNA condensation to fit the small available volumes of the cell. In eukaryotes, DNA is located in the cell nucleus, as well as small amounts in mitochondria and chloroplasts. In prokaryotes, the DNA is held within an irregularly shaped body in the cytoplasm called the nucleoid. The genetic information in a genome is held within genes, and the complete set of this information in an organism is called its genotype. A gene is a unit of heredity and is a region of DNA that influences a particular characteristic in an organism. Genes contain an open reading frame that can be transcribed, as well as regulatory sequences such as promoters and enhancers, which control the transcription of the open reading frame.

In many species, only a small fraction of the total sequence of the genome encodes protein. For example, only about 1.5 per cent of the human genome consists of protein-coding exons, with over 50 per cent of human DNA consisting of non-coding repetitive sequences. The reasons for the presence of so much non-coding DNA in eukaryotic genomes and the extraordinary differences in genome size, or *C-value*, among species represent a long-standing puzzle known as the 'C-value enigma'. However, DNA sequences that do not code protein may still encode functional non-coding RNA molecules, which are involved in the regulation of gene expression.

Some non-coding DNA sequences play structural roles in chromosomes. Telomeres and centromeres typically contain few genes, but are important for the function and stability of chromosomes. An abundant form of non-coding DNA in humans are pseudogenes, which are copies of genes that have been disabled by mutation. These sequences are usually just molecular fossils, although they can occasionally serve as raw genetic material for the creation of new genes through the process of gene duplication and divergence.

Transcription and Translation

A gene is a sequence of DNA that contains genetic information and can influence the phenotype of an organism. Within a gene, the sequence of bases along a DNA strand defines a messenger RNA sequence, which then defines one or more protein sequences. The relationship between the nucleotide sequences of genes and the amino-acid sequences of proteins is determined by the rules of translation, known collectively as the genetic code. The genetic code consists of three-letter 'words' called *codons* formed from a sequence of three nucleotides (e.g. ACT, CAG, TTT).

In transcription, the codons of a gene are copied into messenger RNA by RNA polymerase. This RNA copy is then decoded by a ribosome that reads the RNA sequence by base-pairing the messenger RNA to transfer RNA, which carries amino acids. Since there are 4 bases in 3-letter combinations, there are 64 possible codons (4^3 combinations). These encode the twenty standard amino acids, giving most amino acids more than one possible codon. There are also three 'stop' or 'nonsense' codons signifying the end of the coding region; these are the TAA, TGA and TAG codons.

Replication

Cell division is essential for an organism to grow, but, when a cell divides, it must replicate the DNA in its genome so that the two daughter cells have the same genetic information as their parent. The double-stranded structure of DNA provides a simple mechanism for DNA replication. Here, the two strands are separated and then each strand's complementary DNA sequence is recreated by an enzyme called DNA polymerase. This enzyme makes the complementary strand by finding the correct base through complementary base pairing, and bonding it onto the original strand. As DNA polymerases can only extend a DNA strand in a 5' to 3' direction, different mechanisms are used to copy the antiparallel strands of the double helix. In this way, the base on the old strand dictates which base appears on the new strand, and the cell ends up with a perfect copy of its DNA.

DNA-binding Proteins

Structural proteins that bind DNA are well-understood examples of non-specific DNA-protein interactions. Within chromosomes, DNA is held in complexes with structural proteins. These proteins organize the DNA into a compact structure called chromatin. In eukaryotes this structure involves DNA binding to a complex of small basic proteins called histones, while in prokaryotes multiple types of proteins are involved. The histones form a disk-shaped complex called a nucleosome, which contains two complete turns of double-stranded DNA wrapped around its surface. These non-specific interactions are formed through basic residues in the histones making ionic bonds to the acidic sugar-phosphate backbone of the DNA, and are therefore largely independent of the base sequence. Chemical modifications of these basic amino acid residues include methylation, phosphorylation and acetylation. These chemical changes alter the strength of the interaction between the DNA and the histones, making the DNA more or less accessible to transcription factors and changing the rate of transcription. Other non-specific DNA-binding proteins in chromatin include the high-mobility group proteins, which bind to bent or distorted DNA. These proteins are important in bending arrays of nucleosomes and arranging them into the larger structures that make up chromosomes.

A distinct group of DNA-binding proteins are the DNA-binding proteins that specifically bind single-stranded DNA. In humans, replication protein A is the best-understood member of this family and is used in processes where the double helix is separated, including DNA replication, recombination and DNA repair. These binding proteins seem to stabilize single-stranded DNA and protect it from forming stem-loops or being degraded by nucleases.

In contrast, other proteins have evolved to bind to particular DNA sequences. The most intensively studied of these are the various transcription factors, which are proteins that regulate transcription. Each transcription factor binds to one particular set of DNA sequences and activates or inhibits the transcription of genes that have these sequences close to their promoters. The transcription factors do this in two ways. Firstly, they can bind the RNA polymerase responsible for transcription, either directly or through other mediator proteins; this locates the polymerase at the promoter and allows it to begin transcription. Alternatively, transcription factors can bind enzymes that modify the histones at the promoter; this will change the accessibility of the DNA template to the polymerase.

As these DNA targets can occur throughout an organism's genome, changes in the activity of one type of transcription factor can affect thousands of genes. Consequently, these proteins are often the targets of the signal transduction processes that control responses to environmental changes or cellular differentiation and development. The specificity of these transcription factors' interactions with DNA come from the proteins making multiple contacts to the edges of the DNA bases, allowing them to 'read' the DNA sequence. Most of these base-interactions are made in the major groove, where the bases are most accessible.

Nucleases and Ligases

Nucleases are enzymes that cut DNA strands by catalyzing the hydrolysis of the phosphodiester bonds. Nucleases that hydrolyse nucleotides from the ends of DNA strands are called exonucleases, while endonucleases cut within strands. The most frequently used nucleases in molecular biology are the restriction endonucleases, which cut DNA at specific sequences. For instance, the EcoRV enzyme shown to the left recognizes the 6-base sequence 5'-GAT|ATC-3' and makes a cut at the vertical line. In nature, these enzymes protect bacteria against phage infection by digesting the phage DNA when it enters the bacterial cell, acting as part of the restriction modification system. In technology, these sequence-specific nucleases are used in molecular cloning and DNA fingerprinting.

Enzymes called DNA ligases can rejoin cut or broken DNA strands. Ligases are particularly important in lagging strand DNA replication, as they join together the short segments of DNA produced at the replication fork into a complete copy of the DNA template. They are also used in DNA repair and genetic recombination.

Topoisomerases and Helicases

Topoisomerases are enzymes with both nuclease and ligase activity. These proteins change the amount of supercoiling in DNA. Some of these enzymes work by cutting the DNA helix and allowing one section to rotate, thereby reducing its level of supercoiling; the enzyme then seals the DNA break. Other types of these enzymes are capable of cutting one DNA helix and then passing a second strand of DNA through this break, before rejoining the helix. Topoisomerases are required for many processes involving DNA, such as DNA replication and transcription.

Helicases are proteins that are a type of molecular motor. They use the chemical energy in nucleoside triphosphates, predominantly ATP, to break hydrogen bonds between bases and unwind the DNA double helix into single strands. These enzymes are essential for most processes where enzymes need to access the DNA bases.

Polymerases

Polymerases are enzymes that synthesize polynucleotide chains from nucleoside triphosphates. The sequence of their products are copies of existing polynucleotide chains — which are called *templates*. These enzymes function by adding nucleotides onto the 3′ hydroxyl group of the previous nucleotide in a DNA strand. As a consequence, all polymerases work in a 5′ to 3′ direction. In the active site of these enzymes, the incoming nucleoside triphosphate base-pairs to the template: this allows polymerases to accurately synthesize the complementary strand of their template. Polymerases are classified according to the type of template that they use.

In DNA replication, a DNA-dependent DNA polymerase makes a copy of a DNA sequence. Accuracy is vital in this process, so many of these polymerases have a proofreading activity. Here, the polymerase recognizes the occasional mistakes in the synthesis reaction by the lack of base pairing between the mismatched nucleotides. If a mismatch is detected, a 3′ to 5′ exonuclease activity is activated and the incorrect base removed. In most organisms, DNA polymerases function in a large complex called the replisome that contains multiple accessory subunits, such as the DNA clamp or helicases.

RNA-dependent DNA polymerases are a specialized class of polymerases that copy the sequence of an RNA strand into DNA. They include reverse transcriptase, which is a viral enzyme involved in the infection of cells by retroviruses, and telomerase, which is required for the replication of telomeres. Telomerase is an unusual polymerase because it contains its own RNA template as part of its structure.

Transcription is carried out by a DNA-dependent RNA polymerase that copies the sequence of a DNA strand into RNA. To begin transcribing a gene, the RNA polymerase binds to a sequence of DNA called a promoter and separates the DNA strands. It then copies the gene sequence into a messenger RNA transcript until it reaches a region of DNA called the terminator, where it halts and detaches from the DNA. As with human DNA-dependent DNA polymerases, RNA polymerase II, the enzyme that transcribes most of the genes in the human genome, operates as part of a large protein complex with multiple regulatory and accessory subunits.

A DNA helix usually does not interact with other segments of DNA, and in human cells the different chromosomes even occupy separate areas in the nucleus called 'chromosome territories'. This physical separation of different chromosomes is important for the ability of DNA to function as a stable repository for information, as one of the few times chromosomes interact is during chromosomal crossover when they recombine. Chromosomal crossover is when two DNA helices break, swap a section and then rejoin.

Recombination allows chromosomes to exchange genetic information and produces new combinations of genes, which increases the efficiency of natural selection and can be important in the rapid evolution of new proteins. Genetic recombination can also be involved in DNA repair, particularly in the cell's response to double-strand breaks.

The most common form of chromosomal crossover is homologous recombination, where the two chromosomes involved share very similar sequences. Non-homologous recombination can be damaging to cells, as it can produce chromosomal translocations and genetic abnormalities. The recombination reaction is catalyzed by enzymes known as recombinases, such as RAD51. The first step in recombination is a double-stranded break either caused by an endonuclease or damage to the DNA. A series of steps catalyzed in part by the recombinase then leads to joining of the two helices by at least one Holliday junction, in which a segment of a single strand in each helix is annealed to the complementary strand in the other helix. The Holliday junction is a tetrahedral junction structure that can be moved along the pair of chromosomes, swapping one strand for another. The recombination reaction is then halted by cleavage of the junction and re-ligation of the released DNA.

Evolution

DNA contains the genetic information that allows all modern living things to function, grow and reproduce. However, it is unclear how long in the 4-billion-year history of life DNA has performed this function, as it has been proposed that the earliest forms of life may have used RNA as their genetic material. RNA may have acted as the central part of early cell metabolism as it can both transmit genetic information and carry out catalysis as part of ribozymes. This ancient RNA world where nucleic acid would have been used for both catalysis and genetics may have influenced the evolution of the current genetic code based on four nucleotide bases. This would occur, since the number of different bases in such an organism is a trade-off between a small number of bases increasing replication accuracy and a large number of bases increasing the catalytic efficiency of ribozymes.

However, there is no direct evidence of ancient genetic systems, as recovery of DNA from most fossils is impossible. This is because DNA will survive in the environment for less than one million years and slowly degrades into short fragments in solution. Claims for older DNA have been made, most notably a report of the isolation of a viable bacterium from a salt crystal 250 million years old, but these claims are controversial.

Uses in Technology

Genetic engineering, also called genetic modification, is the direct human manipulation of an organism's genetic material in a way that does not occur under natural conditions. It involves the use of recombinant DNA techniques, but does not include traditional animal and plant breeding or mutagenesis. Any organism that is generated using these techniques is considered to be a genetically modified organism. The first organisms genetically engineered were bacteria in 1973 and then mice in 1974. Insulin producing bacteria were commercialized in 1982 and genetically modified food has been sold since 1994.

Producing genetically modified organisms is a multi-step process. It first involves the isolating and copying the genetic material of interest. A construct is built containing all the genetic elements for correct expression. This construct is then inserted into the host organism, either by using a vector or directly through injection, in a process called transformation. Successfully transformed organisms are then grown and the presence of the new genetic material is tested for.

Genetic engineering techniques have been applied to various industries, with some success. Medicines such as insulin and human growth hormone are now produced in bacteria, experimental mice such as the oncomouse and the knockout mouse are being used for research purposes and insect resistant and/or herbicide tolerant crops have been commercialized. Plants that contain drugs and vaccines, animals with beneficial proteins in their milk and stress tolerant crops are currently being developed.

Forensics

Forensic scientists can use DNA in blood, semen, skin, saliva or hair found at a crime scene to identify a matching DNA of an individual, such as a perpetrator. This process is formally termed DNA profiling, but may also be called 'genetic fingerprinting'. In DNA profiling, the lengths of variable sections of repetitive DNA, such as short tandem repeats and minisatellites, are compared between people. This method is usually an extremely reliable technique for identifying a matching DNA. However, identification can be complicated if the scene is contaminated with DNA from several people. DNA profiling was developed in 1984 by British geneticist Sir Alec Jeffreys, and first used in forensic science to convict Colin Pitchfork in the 1988 Enderby murders case.

People convicted of certain types of crimes may be required to provide a sample of DNA for a database. This has helped investigators solve old cases where only a DNA sample was obtained from the scene. DNA profiling can also be used to identify victims of mass casualty incidents. On the other hand, many convicted people have been released from prison on the basis of DNA techniques, which were not available when a crime had originally been committed.

Bioinformatics

Bioinformatics involves the manipulation, searching, and data mining of DNA sequence data. The development of techniques to store and search DNA sequences have led to widely applied advances in computer science, especially string searching algorithms, machine learning and database theory. String searching or matching algorithms, which find an occurrence of a sequence of letters inside a larger sequence of letters, were developed to search for specific sequences of nucleotides. In other applications such as text editors, even simple algorithms for this problem usually suffice, but DNA sequences cause these algorithms to exhibit near-worst-case behaviour due to their small number of distinct characters.

The related problem of sequence alignment aims to identify homologous sequences and locate the specific mutations that make them distinct. These techniques, especially multiple sequence alignment, are used in studying phylogenetic relationships and protein function. Data sets representing entire genomes' worth of DNA sequences, such as those produced by the Human Genome Project, are difficult to use without annotations, which label the locations of genes and regulatory elements on each chromosome. Regions of DNA sequence that have the characteristic patterns associated with protein — or RNA-coding genes can be identified by gene finding algorithms, which allow researchers to predict the presence of particular gene products in an organism even before they have been isolated experimentally.

DNA Nanotechnology

DNA nanotechnology uses the unique molecular recognition properties of DNA and other nucleic acids to create self-assembling branched DNA complexes with useful properties. DNA is thus used as a structural material rather than as a carrier of biological information. This has led to the creation of two-dimensional periodic lattices (both tile-based as well as using the 'DNA origami' method) as well as three-dimensional structures in the shapes of polyhedra Nanomechanical devices and algorithmic self-assembly have also been demonstrated, and these DNA structures have been used to template the arrangement of other molecules such as gold nanoparticles and streptavidin proteins.

Because DNA collects mutations over time, which are then inherited, it contains historical information, and, by comparing DNA sequences, geneticists can infer the evolutionary history of organisms, their phylogeny. This field of phylogenetics is a powerful tool in evolutionary biology. If DNA sequences within a species are compared, population geneticists can learn the history of particular populations. This can be used in studies ranging from ecological genetics to anthropology; For example, DNA evidence is being used to try to identify the Ten Lost Tribes of Israel.

DNA has also been used to look at modern family relationships, such as establishing family relationships between the descendants of Sally Hemings and Thomas Jefferson. This usage is closely related to the use of DNA in criminal investigations detailed above. Indeed, some criminal investigations have been solved when DNA from crime scenes has matched relatives of the guilty individual.

DNA was first isolated by the Swiss physician Friedrich Miescher who, in 1869, discovered a microscopic substance in the pus of discarded surgical bandages. As it resided in the nuclei of cells, he called it 'nuclein'. In 1919, Phoebus Levene identified the base, sugar and phosphate nucleotide unit. Levene suggested that DNA consisted of a string of nucleotide units linked together through the phosphate groups. However, Levene thought the chain was short and the bases repeated in a fixed order. In 1937 William Astbury produced the first X-ray diffraction patterns that showed that DNA had a regular structure.

In 1928, Frederick Griffith discovered that traits of the 'smooth' form of the *Pneumococcus* could be transferred to the 'rough' form of the same bacteria by mixing killed 'smooth' bacteria with the live 'rough' form. This system provided the first clear suggestion that DNA carries genetic information—the Avery–MacLeod–McCarty experiment—when Oswald Avery, along with coworkers Colin MacLeod and Maclyn McCarty, identified DNA as the transforming principle in 1943. DNA's role in heredity was confirmed in 1952, when Alfred Hershey and Martha Chase in the Hershey–Chase experiment showed that DNA is the genetic material of the T2 phage.

In 1953, James D. Watson and Francis Crick suggested what is now accepted as the first correct double-helix model of DNA structure in the journal *Nature*. Their double-helix, molecular model of DNA was then based on a single X-ray diffraction image (labeled as 'Photo 51') taken by Rosalind Franklin and Raymond Gosling in May 1952, as well as the information that the DNA bases are paired – also obtained through private communications from Erwin Chargaff in the previous years. Chargaff's rules played a very important role in establishing double-helix configurations for B-DNA as well as A-DNA.

Experimental evidence supporting the Watson and Crick model were published in a series of five articles in the same issue of *Nature*. Of these, Franklin and Gosling's paper was the first publication of their own X-ray diffraction data and original analysis method that partially supported the Watson and Crick model ; this issue also contained an article on DNA structure by Maurice Wilkins and two of his colleagues, whose analysis and *in vivo* B-DNA X-ray patterns also supported the presence *in vivo* of the double-helical DNA configurations as proposed by Crick and Watson for their double-helix molecular model of DNA in the previous two pages of *Nature*. In 1962, after Franklin's death, Watson, Crick, and Wilkins jointly received the Nobel Prize in Physiology or Medicine. However, Nobel rules of the time allowed only living recipients, but a vigorous debate continues on who should receive credit for the discovery.

In an influential presentation in 1957, Crick laid out the central dogma of molecular biology, which foretold the relationship between DNA, RNA, and proteins, and articulated the 'adaptor hypothesis'. Final confirmation of the replication mechanism that was implied by the double-helical structure followed in 1958 through the Meselson–Stahl experiment. Further work by Crick and co-workers showed that the genetic code was based on non-overlapping triplets of bases, called codons, allowing Har Gobind Khorana, Robert W. Holley and Marshall Warren Nirenberg to decipher the genetic code. These findings represent the birth of molecular biology.

Chromosome

A *chromosome* is an organized structure of DNA and protein that is found in cells. It is a single piece of coiled DNA containing many genes, regulatory elements and other nucleotide sequences. Chromosomes also contain DNA-bound proteins, which serve to package the DNA and control its functions. The word *chromosome* comes from the Greek (*chroma,* colour) and (*soma,* body) due to their property of being very strongly stained by particular dyes.

Chromosomes vary widely between different organisms. The DNA molecule may be circular or linear, and can be composed of 10,000 to 1,000,000,000 nucleotides in a long chain. Typically eukaryotic cells (cells with nuclei) have large linear chromosomes and prokaryotic cells (cells without defined nuclei) have smaller circular chromosomes, although there are many exceptions to this rule. Furthermore, cells may contain more than one type of chromosome; for example, mitochondria in most eukaryotes and chloroplasts in plants have their own small chromosomes. In eukaryotes, nuclear chromosomes are packaged by proteins into a condensed structure called chromatin. This allows the very long DNA molecules to fit into the cell nucleus. The structure of chromosomes and chromatin varies through the cell cycle. Chromosomes are the essential unit for cellular division and must be replicated, divided, and passed successfully to their daughter cells so as to ensure the genetic diversity and survival of their progeny. Chromosomes may exist as either duplicated or unduplicated—unduplicated chromosomes are single linear strands, whereas duplicated chromosomes (copied during synthesis phase) contain two copies joined by a centromere. Compaction of the duplicated chromosomes during mitosis and meiosis results in the classic four-arm structure (pictured to the right). Chromosomal recombination plays a vital role in genetic diversity. If these structures are manipulated incorrectly, through processes known as chromosomal instability and translocation, the cell may undergo mitotic catastrophe and die, or it may aberrantly evade apoptosis leading to the progression of cancer.

In practice 'chromosome' is a rather loosely defined term. In prokaryotes and viruses, the term genophore is more appropriate when no chromatin is present. However, a large body of work uses the term chromosome regardless of chromatin content. In prokaryotes DNA is usually arranged as a circle, which is tightly coiled in on itself, sometimes accompanied by one or more smaller, circular DNA molecules called plasmids. These small circular genomes are also found in mitochondria and chloroplasts, reflecting their bacterial origins. The simplest genophores are found in viruses: these DNA or RNA molecules are short linear or circular genophores that often lack structural proteins.

In a series of experiments, Theodor Boveri gave the definitive demonstration that chromosomes are the vectors of heredity. His two principles were based upon the *continuity* of chromosomes and the *individuality* of chromosomes . It is the second of these principles that was so original . Boveri was able to test the proposal put forward by Wilhelm Roux, that each chromosome carries a different genetic load, and showed that Roux was right. Upon the rediscovery of Mendel, Boveri was able to point out the connection between the rules of inheritance and the behaviour of the chromosomes. It is interesting to see that Boveri influenced two generations of American cytologists: Edmund Beecher Wilson, Walter Sutton and Theophilus Painter were all influenced by Boveri (Wilson and Painter actually worked with him).

In his famous textbook *The Cell,* Wilson linked Boveri and Sutton together by the Boveri-Sutton theory. Mayr remarks that the theory was hotly contested by some famous geneticists: William Bateson, Wilhelm Johannsen, Richard Goldschmidt and T.H. Morgan, all of a rather dogmatic turn-of-mind. Eventually complete proof came from chromosome maps in Morgan's own lab.

Chromosomes in Eukaryotes

Eukaryotes (cells with nuclei such as those found in plants, yeast, and animals) possess multiple large linear chromosomes contained in the cell's nucleus. Each chromosome has one centromere, with one or two arms projecting from the centromere, although, under most circumstances, these arms are not visible as such. In addition, most eukaryotes have a small circular mitochondrial genome, and some eukaryotes may have additional small circular or linear cytoplasmic chromosomes.

In the nuclear chromosomes of eukaryotes, the uncondensed DNA exists in a semi-ordered structure, where it is wrapped around histones (structural proteins), forming a composite material called chromatin.

Chromatin

Chromatin is the complex of DNA and protein found in the eukaryotic nucleus, which packages chromosomes. The structure of chromatin varies significantly between different stages of the cell cycle, according to the requirements of the DNA.

Interphase Chromatin

During interphase (the period of the cell cycle where the cell is not dividing), two types of chromatin can be distinguished:

- Euchromatin, which consists of DNA that is active, e.g., being expressed as protein.
- Heterochromatin, which consists of mostly inactive DNA. It seems to serve structural purposes during the chromosomal stages. Heterochromatin can be further distinguished into two types:
  1. *Constitutive heterochromatin,* which is never expressed. It is located around the centromere and usually contains repetitive sequences.
  2. *Facultative heterochromatin,* which is sometimes expressed.

Individual chromosomes cannot be distinguished at this stage — they appear in the nucleus as a homogeneous tangled mix of DNA and protein.

In the early stages of mitosis or meiosis (cell division), the chromatin strands become more and more condensed. They cease to function as accessible genetic material (transcription stops) and become a compact transportable form. This compact form makes the individual chromosomes visible, and they form the classic four arm structure, a pair of sister chromatids attached to each other at the centromere. The shorter arms are called *p arms* (from the French *petit,* small) and the longer arms are called *q arms* (*q* follows *p* in the Latin alphabet). This is the only natural context in which individual chromosomes are visible with an optical microscope.

During divisions, long microtubules attach to the centromere and the two opposite ends of the cell. The microtubules then pull the chromatids apart, so that each daughter cell inherits one set of chromatids. Once the cells have divided, the chromatids are uncoiled and can function again as chromatin. In spite of their appearance, chromosomes are structurally highly condensed, which enables these giant DNA structures to be contained within a cell nucleus.

The self-assembled microtubules form the spindle, which attaches to chromosomes at specialized structures called kinetochores, one of which is present on each sister chromatid. A special DNA base sequence in the region of the kinetochores provides, along with special proteins, longer-lasting attachment in this region.

Chromosomes in Prokaryotes

The prokaryotes — bacteria and archaea — typically have a single circular chromosome, but many variations do exist Most bacteria have a single circular chromosome that can range in size from only 160,000 base pairs in the endosymbiotic bacterium *Candidatus Carsonella ruddii*, to 12,200,000 base pairs in the soil-dwelling bacterium *Sorangium cellulosum*. Spirochaetes of the genus *Borrelia* are a notable exception to this arrangement, with bacteria such as *Borrelia burgdorferi*, the cause of Lyme disease, containing a single linear chromosome.

Structure in Sequences

Prokaryotic chromosomes have less sequence-based structure than eukaryotes. Bacteria typically have a single point (the origin of replication) from which replication starts, whereas some archaea contain multiple replication origins. The genes in prokaryotes are often organized in operons, and do not usually contain introns, unlike eukaryotes.

DNA Packaging

Prokaryotes do not possess nuclei. Instead, their DNA is organized into a structure called the nucleoid. The nucleoid is a distinct structure and occupies a defined region of the bacterial cell. This structure is, however, dynamic and is maintained and remodelled by the actions of a range of histone-like proteins, which associate with the bacterial chromosome. In archaea, the DNA in chromosomes is even more organized, with the DNA packaged within structures similar to eukaryotic nucleosomes.

Bacterial chromosomes tend to be tethered to the plasma membrane of the bacteria. In molecular biology application, this allows for its isolation from plasmid DNA by centrifugation of lysed bacteria and pelleting of the membranes (and the attached DNA).

Prokaryotic chromosomes and plasmids are, like eukaryotic DNA, generally supercoiled. The DNA must first be released into its relaxed state for access for transcription, regulation, and replication.

Normal members of a particular eukaryotic species all have the same number of nuclear chromosomes . Other eukaryotic chromosomes, i.e., mitochondrial and plasmid-like small chromosomes, are much more variable in number, and there may be thousands of copies per cell.

Asexually reproducing species have one set of chromosomes, which are the same in all body cells. However, asexual species can be either haploid or diploid.

Sexually reproducing species have somatic cells (body cells), which are diploid [2*n*] having two sets of chromosomes, one from the mother and one from the father. Gametes, reproductive cells, are haploid [*n*]: They have one set of chromosomes. Gametes are produced by meiosis of a diploid germ line cell. During meiosis, the matching chromosomes of father and mother can exchange small parts of themselves (crossover), and thus create new chromosomes that are not inherited solely from either parent. When a male and a female gamete merge (fertilization), a new diploid organism is formed.

Some animal and plant species are polyploid [*Xn*]: They have more than two sets of homologous chromosomes.

Plants important in agriculture such as tobacco or wheat are often polyploid, compared to their ancestral species. Wheat has a haploid number of seven chromosomes, still seen in some cultivars as well as the wild progenitors. The more-common pasta and bread wheats are polyploid, having 28 (tetraploid) and 42 (hexaploid) chromosomes, compared to the 14 (diploid) chromosomes in the wild wheat.

Prokaryotes

Prokaryote species generally have one copy of each major chromosome, but most cells can easily survive with multiple copies. For example, *Buchnera,* a symbiont of aphids has multiple copies of its chromosome, ranging from 10-400 copies per cell. However, in some large bacteria, such as *Epulopiscium fishelsoni* up to 100,000 copies of the chromosome can be present. Plasmids and plasmid-like small chromosomes are, as in eukaryotes, very variable in copy number. The number of plasmids in the cell is almost entirely determined by the rate of division of the plasmid — fast division causes high copy number, and vice versa.

Karyotype

In general, the karyotype is the characteristic chromosome complement of a eukaryote species. The preparation and study of karyotypes is part of cytogenetics.

Although the replication and transcription of DNA is highly standardized in eukaryotes, *the same cannot be said for their karyotypes,* which are often highly variable. There may be variation between species in chromosome number and in detailed organization. In some cases, there is significant variation within species. Often there is:

1. variation between the two sexes.
2. variation between the germ-line and soma (between gametes and the rest of the body).
3. variation between members of a population, due to balanced genetic polymorphism.

4. geographical variation between races.
5. mosaics or otherwise abnormal individuals.

Also, variation in karyotype may occur during development from the fertilised egg.

The technique of determining the karyotype is usually called *karyotyping*. Cells can be locked part-way through division (in metaphase) in vitro (in a reaction vial) with colchicine. These cells are then stained, photographed, and arranged into a *karyogram,* with the set of chromosomes arranged, autosomes in order of length, and sex chromosomes (here *X/Y*) at the end:

Like many sexually reproducing species, humans have special gonosomes (sex chromosomes, in contrast to autosomes). These are *XX* in females and *XY* in males.

Investigation into the human karyotype took many years to settle the most basic question. How many chromosomes does a normal diploid human cell contain? In 1912, Hans von Winiwarter reported 47 chromosomes in spermatogonia and 48 in oogonia, concluding an *XX/XO* sex determination mechanism. Painter in 1922 was not certain whether the diploid number of man is 46 or 48, at first favouring 46. He revised his opinion later from 46 to 48, and he correctly insisted on man's having an *XX/XY* system.

New techniques were needed to definitively solve the problem:

1. Using cells in culture.
2. Pretreating cells in a hypotonic solution, which swells them and spreads the chromosomes.
3. Arresting mitosis in metaphase by a solution of colchicine.
4. Squashing the preparation on the slide forcing the chromosomes into a single plane.
5. Cutting up a photomicrograph and arranging the result into an indisputable karyogram.

It took until the mid-1950s for it to become generally accepted that the human karyotype include only 46 chromosomes. Considering the techniques of Winiwarter and Painter, their results were quite remarkable. Chimpanzees (the closest living relatives to modern humans) have 48 chromosomes.

Chromosomal Aberrations

The three major single chromosome mutations:

1. deletion;
2. duplication; and
3. inversion.

The two major two-chromosome mutations:

1. insertion; and
2. translocation.

Chromosomal aberrations are disruptions in the normal chromosomal content of a cell, and are a major cause of genetic conditions in humans, such as Down syndrome. Some chromosome abnormalities do not cause disease in carriers, such as translocations, or chromosomal inversions, although they may lead to a higher chance of birthing a child with a chromosome disorder. Abnormal numbers of chromosomes or chromosome sets, aneuploidy, may be lethal or give rise to genetic disorders. Genetic counseling is offered for families that may carry a chromosome rearrangement.

The gain or loss of DNA from chromosomes can lead to a variety of genetic disorders. Human examples include:

- Cri du chat, which is caused by the deletion of part of the short arm of chromosome 5. 'Cri du chat' means 'cry of the cat' in French, and the condition was so-named because affected babies make high-pitched cries that sound like those of a cat. Affected individuals have wide-set eyes, a small head and jaw, moderate to severe mental health issues, and are very short.

- Down syndrome, usually is caused by an extra copy of chromosome 21 (trisomy 21). Characteristics include decreased muscle tone, stockier build, asymmetrical skull, slanting eyes and mild to moderate developmental disability.

Edwards syndrome, which is the second-most-common trisomy; Down syndrome is the most common. It is a trisomy of chromosome 18. Symptoms include motor retardation, developmental disability and numerous congenital anomalies causing serious health problems. Ninety per cent die in infancy; however, those that live past their first birthday usually are quite healthy thereafter. They have a characteristic clenched hands and overlapping fingers. Idic15, abbreviation for Isodicentric 15 on chromosome 15; also called the following names due to various researches, but they all mean the same; IDIC(15), Inverted duplication 15, extra Marker, Inv dup 15, partial tetrasomy 15 Jacobsen syndrome, also called the terminal 11q deletion disorder. This is a very rare disorder. Those affected have normal intelligence or mild developmental disability, with poor expressive language skills. Most have a bleeding disorder called Paris-Trousseau syndrome. Klinefelter's syndrome (*XXY*). Men with Klinefelter syndrome are usually sterile, and tend to have longer arms and legs and to be taller than their peers. Boys with the syndrome are often shy and quiet, and have a higher incidence of speech delay and dyslexia. During puberty, without testosterone treatment, some of them may develop gynecomastia. Patau Syndrome, also called D-Syndrome or trisomy-13. Symptoms are somewhat similar to those of trisomy-18, but they do not have the characteristic hand shape. Small supernumerary marker chromosome. This means there is an extra, abnormal chromosome. Features depend on the origin of the extra genetic material. Cat-eye syndrome and isodicentric chromosome 15 syndrome (or Idic15) are both caused by a supernumerary marker chromosome, as is Pallister-Killian syndrome. Triple-*X* syndrome (*XXX*). *XXX* girls tend to be tall and thin. They have a higher incidence of dyslexia. Turner syndrome (*X* instead of *XX* or *XY*). In Turner syndrome, female sexual characteristics are present but underdeveloped. People with Turner syndrome often have a short stature, low hairline, abnormal eye features and bone development and a 'caved-in' appearance to the chest. *XYY* syndrome. *XYY* boys are usually taller than their siblings. Like *XXY* boys and *XXX* girls, they are somewhat more likely to have learning difficulties.

Wolf-Hirschhorn syndrome, which is caused by partial deletion of the short arm of chromosome 4. It is characterized by severe growth retardation and severe to profound mental health issues.

Chromosomal mutations produce changes in whole chromosomes (more than one gene) or in the number of chromosomes present.

- ❖ Deletion – loss of part of a chromosome.
- ❖ Duplication – extra copies of a part of a chromosome.
- ❖ Inversion – reverse the direction of a part of a chromosome.
- ❖ Translocation – part of a chromosome breaks off and attaches to another chromosome

Most mutations are neutral – have little or no effect. Chromosomal aberrations are the changes in the structure of chromosomes. It has a great role in evolution. A detailed graphical display of all human chromosomes and the diseases annotated at the correct spot may be found at the Oak Ridge National Laboratory.

Human Chromosomes

Chromosomes can be divided into two types—autosomes, and sex chromosomes. Certain genetic traits are linked to your sex, and are passed on through the sex chromosomes. The autosomes contain the rest of the genetic hereditary information. All act in the same way during cell division. Human cells have 23 pairs of large linear nuclear chromosomes, (22 pairs of autosomes and one pair of sex chromosomes) giving a total of 46 per cell. In addition to these, human cells have many hundreds of copies of the mitochondrial genome. Sequencing of the human genome has provided a great deal of information about each of the chromosomes. Below is a table compiling statistics for the chromosomes, based on the Sanger Institute's human genome information in the Vertebrate Genome Annotation (VEGA) database. Number of genes is an estimate as it is in part based on gene predictions. Total chromosome length is an estimate as well, based on the estimated size of unsequenced heterochromatin regions.

Chromosomal Crossover

Chromosomal crossover (or crossing over) is an exchange of genetic material between homologous chromosomes. It is one of the final phases of genetic recombination, which occurs during prophase I of meiosis (diplotene) in a process called synapsis. Synapsis begins before the synaptonemal complex develops, and is not completed until near the end of prophase I. Crossover usually occurs when matching regions on matching chromosomes break and then reconnect to the other chromosome.

Crossing over was described, in theory, by Thomas Hunt Morgan. He relied on the discovery of the Belgian Professor Frans Alfons Janssens of the University of Leuven who described the phenomenon in 1909 and had called it 'chiasmatypie'. The term *chiasma* is linked if not identical to chromosomal crossover. Morgan immediately saw the great importance of Janssens' cytological interpretation of chiasmata to the experimental results of his research on the heredity of *Drosophila*. The physical basis of crossing over was first demonstrated by Harriet Creighton and Barbara McClintock in 1931.

Meiotic recombination initiates with double-stranded breaks that are introduced into the DNA by the Spo11 protein. One or more exonucleases then digest the 5′ ends generated by the double-stranded breaks to produce 3′ single-stranded DNA tails. The meiosis-specific recombinase Dmc1 and the general recombinase Rad51 coat the single-stranded DNA to form nucleoprotein filaments. The recombinases catalyze invasion of the opposite chromatid by the single-stranded DNA from one end of the break. Next, the 3′ end of the invading DNA primes DNA synthesis, causing displacement of the complementary strand, which subsequently anneals to the single-stranded DNA generated from the other end of the initial double-stranded break. The structure that results is a *cross-strand exchange,* also known as a Holliday junction. The contact between two chromatids that will soon undergo crossing-over is known as a *chiasma.* The Holliday junction is a tetrahedral structure which can be 'pulled' by other recombinases, moving it along the four-stranded structure.

Consequences

In most eukaryotes, a cell carries two copies of each gene, each referred to as an allele. Each parent passes on one allele to each offspring. An individual gamete inherits a complete haploid complement of alleles on chromosomes that are independently selected from each pair of chromatids lined up on the metaphase plate. Without recombination, all alleles for those genes linked together on the same chromosome would be inherited together. Meiotic recombination allows a more independent selection between the two alleles that occupy the positions of single genes, as recombination shuffles the allele content between homologous chromosomes.

Recombination does not have any influence on the statistical probability that another offspring will have the same combination. This theory of 'independent assortment' of alleles is fundamental to genetic inheritance. However, there is ar exception that requires further discussion.

The frequency of recombination is actually not the same for all gene combinations. This leads to the notion of 'genetic distance', which is a measure of recombination frequency averaged over a (suitably large) sample of pedigrees. Loosely speaking, one may say that this is because recombination is greatly influenced by the proximity of one gene to another. If two genes are located close together on a chromosome, the likelihood that a recombination event will separate these two genes is less than if they were farther apart. Genetic linkage describes the tendency of genes to be inherited together as a result of their location on the same chromosome. Linkage disequilibrium describes a situation in which some combinations of genes or genetic markers occur more or less frequently in a population than would be expected from their distances apart. This concept is applied when searching for a gene that may cause a particular disease. This is done by comparing the occurrence of a specific DNA sequence with the appearance of a disease. When a high correlation between the two is found, it is likely that the appropriate gene sequence is really closer.

Problems

Although crossovers typically occur between homologous regions of matching chromosomes, similarities in sequence can result in mismatched alignments. These processes are called unbalanced recombination. Unbalanced recombination is fairly rare compared to normal recombination, but severe problems can arise if a gamete containing unbalanced recombinants becomes part of a zygote. The result can be a local duplication of genes on one chromosome and a deletion of these on the other, a translocation of part of one chromosome onto a different one, or an inversion.

Regulation of Gene Expression

Regulation of gene expression (or gene regulation) includes the processes that cells and viruses use to regulate the way that the information in genes is turned into gene products. Although a functional gene product may be an RNA or a protein, the majority of known mechanisms regulate protein coding genes. Any step of the gene's expression may be modulated, from DNA-RNA transcription to the post-translational modification of a protein.

Gene regulation is essential for viruses, prokaryotes and eukaryotes as it increases the versatility and adaptability of an organism by allowing the cell to express protein when needed. The first discovered example of a gene regulation system was the lac operon, discovered by Jacques Monod, in which protein involved in lactose metabolism are expressed by *E. coli* only in the presence of lactose and absence of glucose.

Furthermore, gene regulation drives the processes of cellular differentiation and morphogenesis, leading to the creation of different cell types in multicellular organisms where the different types of cells may possess different gene expression profiles though they all possess the same genome sequence.

Regulated Stages of Gene Expression

Any step of gene expression may be modulated, from the DNA-RNA transcription step to post-translational modification of a protein. The following is a list of stages where gene expression is regulated, the most extensively utilised point is Transcription Initiation:

- Chromatin domains
- Transcription
- Post-transcriptional modification
- RNA transport
- Translation
- mRNA degradation

Modification of DNA

In eukaryotes, the accessibility of large regions of DNA can depend on its chromatin structure which can be altered as a result of histone modifications which are directed by DNA methylation, ncRNA or DNA binding protein.

Chemical

Methylation of DNA is a common method of gene silencing. DNA is typically methylated by methyltransferase enzymes on cytosine nucleotides in a *CpG* dinucleotide sequence (also called '*CpG* islands' when densely clustered). Analysis of the pattern of methylation in a given region of DNA (which can be a promoter) can be achieved through a method called bisulfite mapping. Methylated cytosine residues are unchanged by the treatment, whereas unmethylated ones are changed to uracil. The differences are analyzed by DNA sequencing or by methods developed to quantify SNPs, such as Pyrosequencing (Biotage) or MassArray (Sequenom), measuring the relative amounts of *C/T* at the *CG* dinucleotide. Abnormal methylation patterns are thought to be involved in carcinogenesis.

Structural

Transcription of DNA is dictated by its structure. In general, the density of its packing is indicative of the frequency of transcription. Octameric protein complexes called nucleosomes are responsible for the amount of supercoiling of DNA, and these complexes can be temporarily modified by processes such as phosphorylation or more permanently modified by processes such as methylation. Such modifications are considered to be responsible for more or less permanent changes in gene expression levels.

Histone acetylation is also an important process in transcription. Histone acetyltransferase enzymes (HATs) such as CREB binding protein also dissociate the DNA from the histone complex, allowing transcription to proceed. Often, DNA methylation and histone deacetylation work together in gene silencing. The combination of the two seems to be a signal for DNA to be packed more densely, lowering gene expression.

Regulation of Transcription

Regulation of transcription controls when transcription occurs and how much RNA is created. Transcription of a gene by RNA polymerase can be regulated by at least five mechanisms:

- *Specificity factors* alter the specificity of RNA polymerase for a given promoter or set of promoters, making it more or less likely to bind to them (i.e. sigma factors used in prokaryotic transcription).
- *Repressors* bind to non-coding sequences on the DNA strand that are close to or overlapping the promoter region, impeding RNA polymerase's progress along the strand, thus impeding the expression of the gene.
- *General transcription factors:* These transcription factors position RNA polymerase at the start of a protein-coding sequence and then release the polymerase to transcribe the mRNA.

- *Activators* enhance the interaction between RNA polymerase and a particular promoter, encouraging the expression of the gene. Activators do this by increasing the attraction of RNA polymerase for the promoter, through interactions with subunits of the RNA polymerase or indirectly by changing the structure of the DNA.
- *Enhancers* are sites on the DNA helix that are bound to by activators in order to loop the DNA bringing a specific promoter to the initiation complex. Enhancers are much more common in eukaryote than prokaryotes, where only a few examples exist (to date).

Post-transcriptional Regulation

After the DNA is transcribed and mRNA is formed there must be some sort of regulation on how much the mRNA is translated into proteins. Cells do this by modulating the capping, splicing, addition of a Poly(*A*) Tail, the sequence-specific nuclear export rates and in several contexts sequestration of the RNA transcript. These processes occur in eukaryotes but not in prokaryotes. This modulation is a result of a protein or transcript which in turn is regulated and may have an affinity for certain sequences.

- *Capping* changes the five prime end of the mRNA to a three prime end by 5′-5′ linkage, which protects the mRNA from 5′ exonuclease, which degrades foreign RNA. The cap also helps in ribosomal binding.
- *Splicing* removes the introns, noncoding regions that are transcribed into RNA, in order to make the mRNA able to create proteins. Cells do this by spliceosomes binding on either side of an intron, looping the intron into a circle and then cleaving it off. The two ends of the exons are then joined together.
- *Addition of poly(A) tail* otherwise known as poly-adenylation. Junk RNA is added to the 3′ end, and acts as a buffer to the 3′ exonuclease in order to increase the half life of mRNA.

Regulation of Translation

The translation of mRNA can also be controlled by a number of mechanisms, mostly at the level of initiation. Recruitment of the small ribosomal subunit can indeed be modulated by mRNA secondary structure, antisense RNA binding or protein binding. In both prokaryotes and eukaryotes a large number of RNA binding proteins exist, which often are directed to their target sequence by the secondary structure of the transcript, which may change depending on certain conditions, such as temperature or presence of a ligand (aptamer), some transcripts act as ribozymes and self-regulate their expression.

Examples of Gene Regulation

- Enzyme induction is a process in which a molecule (e.g. a drug) induces (i.e. initiates or enhances) the expression of an enzyme.
- The induction of heat shock proteins in the fruit fly *Drosophila melanogaster*.
- The Lac operon is an interesting example of how gene expression can be regulated.
- Viruses despite having only a few genes, possess mechanisms to regulate their gene expression, typically into an early and late phase, using collinear systems regulated by anti-terminators (lambda phage) or splicing modulators (HIV)

Developmental Biology

A large number of studied regulatory systems come from developmental biology. Examples include:

- The colinearity of the Hox gene cluster with their nested antero-posterior patterning
- It has been speculated that pattern generation of the hand (digits - interdigits) The gradient of Sonic hedgehog (secreted inducing factor) from the zone of polarizing activity in the limb which creates a gradient

of active Gli3 which activates Gremlin which inhibits BMPs also secreted in the limb resulting in the formation of an alternating pattern of activity as a result of this reaction-diffusion system.

- Somitogenesis is the creation of segments (somites) from a uniform tissue (Pre-somitic Mesoderm, PSM). They are formed sequentially from anterior to posterior, this is achieved in amniotes possibly by means of two opposing gradients, Retinoic acid in the anterior (wavefront) and *Wnt* and *Fgf* in the posterior, coupled to an oscillating pattern (segmentation clock) composed of *FGF* + Notch and *Wnt* in antiphase.
- Sex determination in the soma of a Drosophila requires the sensing of the ratio of autosomal genes to sex chromosome encoded genes, which results in the production of sexless splicing factor in females resulting in the female isoform of doublesex.

CIRCUITRY

Up-regulation and Down-regulation

Up-regulation is a process which occurs within a cell triggered by a signal (originating internal or external to the cell) which results in increased expression of one or more genes and as a result the protein(s) encoded by those genes. Conversely down-regulation is a process resulting in decreased gene and corresponding protein expression.

Up-regulation occurs for example when a cell is deficient in some kind of receptor. In this case, more receptor protein is synthesized and transported to the membrane of the cell and thus the sensitivity of the cell is brought back to normal reestablishing homeostasis.

Down-regulation occurs for example when a cell is overly stimulated by a neurotransmitter, hormone, or drug for a prolonged period of time and the expression of the receptor protein is decreased in order to protect the cell.

Inducible *vs.* Repressible Systems

Gene Regulation can be summarized as how they respond:

Inducible Dystems: An inducible system is off unless there is the presence of some molecule (called an inducer) that allows for gene expression. The molecule is said to "induce expression". The manner in which this happens is dependent on the control mechanisms as well as differences between prokaryotic and eukaryotic cells.

Repressible Systems: A repressible system is on except in the presence of some molecule (called a corepressor) that suppresses gene expression. The molecule is said to 'repress expression'. The manner in which this happens is dependent on the control mechanisms as well as differences between prokaryotic and eukaryotic cells.

Theoretical Circuits

- Repressor/Inducer: an activation of a sensor results in the change of expression of a gene;
- negative feedback: the gene product downregulates its own production directly or indirectly, which can result in keeping transcript levels constant/proportional to a factor;
- inhibition of run-away reactions when coupled with a positive feedback loop;
- creating an oscillator by taking advantage in the time delay of transcription and translation, given that the mRNA and protein half-life is shorter;
- positive feedback: the gene product upregulates its own production directly or indirectly, which can result in signal amplification;
- bistable switches when two genes inhibit each other and have both positive feedback pattern generation.

Generally, most experiments investigating differential expression used whole cell extracts of RNA, called steady-state levels, to determine which genes changed and by how much they did. These are however not informative of where the regulation has occurred and may actually mask conflicting regulatory processess (*see post-transcriptional regulation*), but it is still the most commonly analysed (QPCR and DNA microarray).

When studying gene expression there are several methods to look at the various stages. In eukaryotes these include:

- The chromatin conformation of the region can be determined by ChIP-chip analysis by pulling down RNA Polymerase II, Histone 3 modifications, Trithorax-group protein, Polycomb-group protein or any other DNA binding element to which a good antibody is available.
- Epistatic interactions can be investigated by synthetic genetic array analysis.
- Due to post-transcriptional regulation, transcription rates and total RNA levels differ significantly, to measure the transcription rates nuclear run-on assays can be done and newer high-throughput methods are being developed, using thiol labelling instead of radioactivity.
- Only 5 per cent of the RNA polymerised in the nucleus actually exists and not only introns, abortive products and non-sense transcripts are degradated therefore the differences in nuclear and cytoplasmic levels can be see by separating the two fractions by gentle lysis.
- Alternative splicing can be analysed with a splicing array or with a tiling array.
- All in vivo RNA is complexed as RNPs. The quantity of transcripts bound to specific protein can be also analysed by RIP-Chip, for example DCP2 will give an indication of sequestered protein, ribosome bound gives and indication of transcripts active in transcription (although it should be noted that a more dated method, called polysome fractionation, is still popular in some labs).

- Protein levels can be analysed by Mass spectrometry, which can only be compare to QPCR data as microarray data is relative and not absolute.
- RNA and protein degradation rates are measured by means of transcription inhibitors (actinomycin *D* or *a*-amanitin) or translation inhibitors (Cycloheximide) respectively.

Natural Selection

Natural selection is the process by which traits become more or less common in a population due to consistent effects upon the survival or reproduction of their bearers. It is a key mechanism of evolution.

The natural genetic variation within a population of organisms may cause some individuals to survive and reproduce more successfully than others in their current environment. For example, the peppered moth exists in both light and dark colours in the United Kingdom, but during the industrial revolution many of the trees on which the moths rested became blackened by soot, giving the dark-coloured moths an advantage in hiding from predators. This gave dark-coloured moths a better chance of surviving to produce dark-coloured offspring, and in just a few generations the majority of the moths were dark. Factors which affect reproductive success are also important, an issue which Charles Darwin developed in his ideas on sexual selection.

Natural selection acts on the phenotype, or the observable characteristics of an organism, but the genetic (heritable) basis of any phenotype which gives a reproductive advantage will become more common in a population. Over time, this process can result in adaptations that specialize populations for particular ecological niches and may eventually result in the emergence of new species. In other words, natural selection is an important process (though not the only process) by which evolution takes place within a population of organisms. As opposed to artificial selection, in which humans favor specific traits, in natural selection the environment acts as a sieve through which only certain variations can pass.

Natural selection is one of the cornerstones of modern biology. The term was introduced by Darwin in his influential 1859 book *On the Origin of Species*, in which natural selection was described as analogous to artificial selection, a process by which animals and plants with traits considered desirable by human breeders are systematically favored for reproduction. The concept of natural selection was originally developed in the absence of a valid theory of heredity; at the time of Darwin's writing, nothing was known of modern genetics. The union of traditional Darwinian evolution with subsequent discoveries in classical and molecular genetics is termed the *modern evolutionary synthesis*. Natural selection remains the primary explanation for adaptive evolution.

Natural variation occurs among the individuals of any population of organisms. Many of these differences do not affect survival (such as differences in eye colour in humans), but some differences may improve the chances of survival of a particular individual. A rabbit that runs faster than others may be more likely to escape from predators, and algae that are more efficient at extracting energy from sunlight will grow faster. Individuals that have better odds for survival also have better odds for reproduction.

If the traits that give these individuals a reproductive advantage are also heritable, that is, passed from parent to child, then there will be a slightly higher proportion of fast rabbits or efficient algae in the next generation. This is known as *differential reproduction*. Even if the reproductive advantage is very slight, over many generations any heritable advantage will become dominant in the population, due to exponential growth. In this way the natural environment of an organism 'selects' for traits that confer a reproductive advantage, causing gradual changes or evolution of life. This effect was first described and named by Charles Darwin.

The concept of natural selection predates the understanding of genetics, which is the study of heredity. In modern times, it is understood that selection acts on an organism's phenotype, or observable characteristics, but it is the organism's genetic make-up or genotype that is inherited. The phenotype is the result of the genotype and the environment in which the organism lives.

This is the link between natural selection and genetics, as described in the modern evolutionary synthesis. Although a complete theory of evolution also requires an account of how genetic variation arises in the first place (such as by mutation and sexual reproduction) and includes other evolutionary mechanisms (such as gene flow), natural selection is still understood as a fundamental mechanism for evolution.

The term *natural selection* has slightly different definitions in different contexts. It is most often defined to operate on heritable traits, because these are the traits that directly participate in evolution. However, natural selection is 'blind' in the sense that changes in phenotype (physical and behavioural characteristics) can give a reproductive advantage regardless of whether or not the trait is heritable (non heritable traits can be the result of environmental factors or the life experience of the organism).

Following Darwin's primary usage the term is often used to refer to both the evolutionary consequence of blind selection and to its mechanisms. It is sometimes helpful to explicitly distinguish between selection's mechanisms and its effects; when this distinction is important, scientists define 'natural selection' specifically as "those mechanisms that contribute to the selection of individuals that reproduce", without regard to whether the basis of the selection is heritable. This is sometimes referred to as 'phenotypic natural selection'.

Traits that cause greater reproductive success of an organism are said to be selected for, whereas those that reduce success are selected against. Selection for a trait may also result in the selection of other correlated traits that do not themselves directly influence reproductive advantage. This may occur as a result of pleiotropy or gene linkage.

Fitness

The concept of fitness is central to natural selection. Broadly, individuals which are more 'fit' have better potential for survival, as in the well-known phrase 'survival of the fittest'. However, as with natural selection above, the precise meaning of the term is much more subtle, and Richard Dawkins manages in his later books to avoid it entirely. (He devotes a chapter of his book, *The Extended Phenotype,* to discuss the various senses in which the term is used). Modern evolutionary theory defines fitness not by how long an organism lives, but by how successful it is at reproducing. If an organism lives half as long as others of its species, but has twice as many offspring surviving to adulthood, its genes will become more common in the adult population of the next generation.

Though natural selection acts on individuals, the effects of chance mean that fitness can only really be defined 'on average' for the individuals within a population. The fitness of a particular genotype corresponds to the average effect on all individuals with that genotype. Very low-fitness genotypes cause their bearers to have few or no offspring on average; examples include many human genetic disorders like cystic fibrosis.

Natural selection can act on any phenotypic trait, and selective pressure can be produced by any aspect of the environment, including sexual selection and competition with members of the same species. However, this does not imply that natural selection is always directional and results in adaptive evolution; natural selection often results in the maintenance of the status quo by eliminating less fit variants.

The unit of selection can be the individual or it can be another level within the hierarchy of biological organisation, such as genes, cells, and kin groups. There is still debate about whether natural selection acts at the level of groups or species to produce adaptations that benefit a larger, non-kin group. Selection at a different level such as the gene can result in an increase in fitness for that gene, while at the same time reducing the fitness of the individuals carrying that gene, in a process called intragenomic conflict. Overall, the combined effect of all selection pressures at various levels determines the overall fitness of an individual, and hence the outcome of natural selection.

The life cycle of a sexually reproducing organism. Various components of natural selection are indicated for each life stage.

Natural selection occurs at every life stage of an individual. An individual organism must survive until adulthood before it can reproduce, and selection of those that reach this stage is called *viability selection*. In many species, adults must compete with each other for mates via sexual selection, and success in this competition determines who will parent the next generation. When individuals can reproduce more than once, a longer survival in the reproductive phase increases the number of offspring, called *survival selection*.

It is useful to distinguish between 'ecological selection' and 'sexual selection'. Ecological selection covers any mechanism of selection as a result of the environment (including relatives, e.g. kin selection, competition, and infanticide), while 'sexual selection' refers specifically to competition for mates.

Sexual selection can be *intrasexual,* as in cases of competition among individuals of the same sex in a population, or *intersexual,* as in cases where one sex controls reproductive access by choosing among a population of available mates. Most commonly, intrasexual selection involves male–male competition and intersexual selection involves female choice of suitable males, due to the generally greater investment of resources for a female than a male in a single offspring. However, some species exhibit sex-role reversed behaviour in which it is males that are most selective in mate choice; the best-known examples of this pattern occur in some fishes of the family *Syngnathidae,* though likely examples have also been found in amphibian and bird species.

Some features that are confined to one sex only of a particular species can be explained by selection exercised by the other sex in the choice of a mate, for example, the extravagant plumage of some male birds. Similarly, aggression between members of the same sex is sometimes associated with very distinctive features, such as the antlers of stags, which are used in combat with other stags. More generally, intrasexual selection is often associated with sexual dimorphism, including differences in body size between males and females of a species.

The fecundity of both females and males (for example, giant sperm in certain species of *Drosophila*) can be limited via 'fecundity selection'. The viability of produced gametes can differ, while intragenomic conflicts such as meiotic drive between the haploid gametes can result in gametic or 'genic selection'. Finally, the union of some combinations of eggs and sperm might be more compatible than others; this is termed *compatibility selection.*

A well-known example of natural selection in action is the development of antibiotic resistance in microorganisms. Since the discovery of penicillin in 1928 by Alexander Fleming, antibiotics have been used to fight bacterial diseases. Natural populations of bacteria contain, among their vast numbers of individual members, considerable variation in their genetic material, primarily as the result of mutations. When exposed to antibiotics, most bacteria die quickly, but some may have mutations that make them slightly less susceptible. If the exposure to antibiotics is short, these individuals will survive the treatment. This selective elimination of maladapted individuals from a population is natural selection.

These surviving bacteria will then reproduce again, producing the next generation. Due to the elimination of the maladapted individuals in the past generation, this population contains more bacteria that have some resistance against the antibiotic. At the same time, new mutations occur, contributing new genetic variation to the existing genetic variation. Spontaneous mutations are very rare, and advantageous mutations are even rarer. However, populations of bacteria are large enough that a few individuals will have beneficial mutations. If a new mutation reduces their susceptibility to an antibiotic, these individuals are more likely to survive when next confronted with that antibiotic.

Given enough time, and repeated exposure to the antibiotic, a population of antibiotic-resistant bacteria will emerge. This new changed population of antibiotic-resistant bacteria is optimally adapted to the context it evolved in. At the same time, it is not necessarily optimally adapted any more to the old antibiotic free environment. The end result of natural selection is two populations that are both optimally adapted to their specific environment, while both perform substandard in the other environment.

The widespread use and misuse of antibiotics has resulted in increased microbial resistance to antibiotics in clinical use, to the point that the methicillin-resistant *Staphylococcus aureus* (MRSA) has been described as a 'superbug' because of the threat it poses to health and its relative invulnerability to existing drugs. Response strategies typically include the use of different, stronger antibiotics; however, new strains of MRSA have recently emerged that are resistant even to these drugs.

This is an example of what is known as an evolutionary arms race, in which bacteria continue to develop strains that are less susceptible to antibiotics, while medical researchers continue to develop new antibiotics that can kill them. A similar situation occurs with pesticide resistance in plants and insects. Arms races are not necessarily induced by man; a well-documented example involves the spread of a gene in the butterfly Hypolimnas bolina suppressing male-killing activity by Wolbachia bacteria parasites on the island of Samoa, where the spread of the gene is known to have occurred over a period of just five years.

A prerequisite for natural selection to result in adaptive evolution, novel traits and speciation, is the presence of heritable genetic variation that results in fitness differences. Genetic variation is the result of mutations, recombinations and alterations in the karyotype (the number, shape, size and internal arrangement of the chromosomes). Any of these changes might have an effect that is highly advantageous or highly disadvantageous, but large effects are very rare. In the past, most changes in the genetic material were considered neutral or close to neutral because they occurred in non-coding DNA or resulted in a synonymous substitution. However, recent research suggests that many mutations in non-coding DNA do have slight deleterious effects. Although both mutation rates and average fitness effects of mutations are dependent on the organism, estimates from data in humans have found that a majority of mutations are slightly deleterious.

The exuberant tail of the peacock is thought to be the result of sexual selection by females. This peacock is an albino; selection against albinos in nature is intense because they are easily spotted by predators or are unsuccessful in competition for mates.

By the definition of fitness, individuals with greater fitness are more likely to contribute offspring to the next generation, while individuals with lesser fitness are more likely to die early or fail to reproduce. As a result, alleles which on average result in greater fitness become more abundant in the next generation, while alleles which generally reduce fitness become rarer. If the selection forces remain the same for many generations, beneficial alleles become more and more abundant, until they dominate the population, while alleles with a lesser fitness disappear. In every generation, new mutations and re-combinations arise spontaneously, producing a new spectrum of phenotypes. Therefore, each new generation will be enriched by the increasing abundance of alleles that contribute to those traits that were favoured by selection, enhancing these traits over successive generations.

Some mutations occur in so-called regulatory genes. Changes in these can have large effects on the phenotype of the individual because they regulate the function of many other genes. Most, but not all, mutations in regulatory genes result in non-viable zygotes. Examples of non-lethal regulatory mutations occur in HOX genes in humans, which can result in a cervical rib or polydactyly, an increase in the number of fingers or toes. When such mutations result in a higher fitness, natural selection will favour these phenotypes and the novel trait will spread in the population.

Established traits are not immutable; traits that have high fitness in one environmental context may be much less fit if environmental conditions change. In the absence of natural selection to preserve such a trait, it will become more variable and deteriorate over time, possibly resulting in a vestigial manifestation of the trait, also called evolutionary baggage. In many circumstances, the apparently vestigial structure may retain a limited functionality, or may be co-opted for other advantageous traits in a phenomenon known as preadaptation. A famous example of a vestigial structure, the eye of the blind mole rat, is believed to retain function in photoperiod perception.

Several ancient philosophers expressed the idea that nature produces a huge variety of creatures, apparently randomly, and that only those creatures survive that manage to provide for themselves and reproduce successfully; well-known examples include Empedocles and his intellectual successor, Lucretius, while related ideas were later refined by Aristotle. The struggle for existence was later described by Al-Jahiz, who argued that environmental factors influence animals to develop new characteristics to ensure survival. Abu Rayhan Biruni described the idea of artificial selection and argued that nature works in much the same way. Similar ideas were later expressed by Nasir al-Din Tusi and Ibn Khaldun. Such classical arguments were reintroduced in the 18th century by Pierre Louis Maupertuis and others, including Charles Darwin's grandfather Erasmus Darwin. While these forerunners had an influence on Darwinism, they later had little influence on the trajectory of evolutionary thought after Charles Darwin.

Until the early 19th century, the prevailing view in Western societies was that differences between individuals of a species were uninteresting departures from their Platonic idealism (or typus) of created kinds. However, the theory of uniformitarianism in geology promoted the idea that simple, weak forces could act continuously over long periods of time to produce radical changes in the Earth's landscape. The success of this theory raised awareness of the vast scale of geological time and made plausible the idea that tiny, virtually imperceptible changes in successive generations could produce consequences on the scale of differences between species. Early 19th century evolutionists such as Jean Baptiste Lamarck suggested the inheritance of acquired characteristics as a mechanism for evolutionary change; adaptive traits acquired by an organism during its lifetime could be inherited by that organism's progeny, eventually causing transmutation of species. This theory has come to be known as Lamarckism and was an influence on the anti-genetic ideas of the Stalinist Soviet biologist Trofim Lysenko.

Darwin's Theory

In 1859, Charles Darwin set out his theory of evolution by natural selection as an explanation for adaptation and speciation. He defined natural selection as the "principle by which each slight variation [of a trait], if useful, is preserved". The concept was simple but powerful: individuals best adapted to their environments are more likely to survive and reproduce. As long as there is some variation between them, there will be an inevitable selection of individuals with the most advantageous variations. If the variations are inherited, then differential reproductive success will lead to a progressive evolution of particular populations of a species, and populations that evolve to be sufficiently different eventually become different species.

Darwin's ideas were inspired by the observations that he had made on the *Beagle* voyage, and by the work of a political economist, the Reverend Thomas Malthus, who in *An Essay on the Principle of Population,* noted that population (if unchecked) increases exponentially whereas the food supply grows only arithmetically; thus inevitable limitations of resources would have demographic implications, leading to a 'struggle for existence'. When Darwin read Malthus in 1838 he was already primed by his work as a naturalist to appreciate the 'struggle for existence' in nature and it struck him that as population outgrew resources, "favourable variations would tend to be preserved, and unfavourable ones to be destroyed. The result of this would be the formation of new species".

Darwin summarised this idea in his book '*On the Origin of Species*': if during the long course of ages and under varying conditions of life, organic beings vary at all in the several parts of their organisation, and I think this cannot be disputed; if there be, owing to the high geometrical powers of increase of each species, at some age, season, or year, a severe struggle for life, and this certainly cannot be disputed;

then, considering the infinite complexity of the relations of all organic beings to each other and to their conditions of existence, causing an infinite diversity in structure, constitution, and habits, to be advantageous to them, I think it would be a most extraordinary fact if no variation ever had occurred useful to each being's own welfare, in the same way as so many variations have occurred useful to man. But if variations useful to any organic being do occur, assuredly individuals thus characterised will have the best chance of being preserved in the struggle for life; and from the strong principle of inheritance they will tend to produce offspring similarly characterised. This principle of preservation, I have called, for the sake of brevity, natural selection".

Once he had his theory 'by which to work', Darwin was meticulous about gathering and refining evidence as his 'prime hobby' before making his idea public. He was in the process of writing his "big book" to present his researches when the naturalist Alfred Russel Wallace independently conceived of the principle and described it in an essay he sent to Darwin to forward to Charles Lyell. Lyell and Joseph Dalton Hooker decided (without Wallace's knowledge) to present his essay together with unpublished writings which Darwin had sent to fellow naturalists, and *On the Tendency of Species to form Varieties; and on the Perpetuation of Varieties and Species by Natural Means of Selection* was read to the Linnean Society announcing co-discovery of the principle in July 1858. Darwin published a detailed account of his evidence and conclusions in *On the Origin of Species* in 1859. In the 3rd edition of 1861 Darwin acknowledged that others — notably William Charles Wells in 1813, and Patrick Matthew in 1831 — had proposed similar ideas, but had neither developed them nor presented them in notable scientific publications.

Darwin thought of natural selection by analogy to how farmers select crops or livestock for breeding, which he called 'artificial selection'; in his early manuscripts he referred to a 'Nature' which would do the selection. At the time, other mechanisms of evolution such as evolution by genetic drift were not yet explicitly formulated, and Darwin believed that selection was likely only part of the story: "I am convinced that [it] has been the main, but not exclusive means of modification." In a letter to Charles Lyell in September 1860, Darwin regretted the use of the term 'Natural Selection', preferring the term "Natural Preservation". For Darwin and his contemporaries, natural selection was essentially synonymous with evolution by natural selection. After the publication of *On the Origin of Species*, educated people generally accepted that evolution had occurred in some form. However, natural selection remained controversial as a mechanism, partly because it was perceived to be too weak to explain the range of observed characteristics of living organisms, and partly because even supporters of evolution balked at its 'unguided' and non-progressive nature, a response that has been characterized as the single most significant impediment to the idea's acceptance. However, some thinkers enthusiastically embraced natural selection; after reading Darwin, Herbert Spencer introduced the term *survival of the fittest*, which became a popular summary of the theory. The fifth edition of *On the Origin of Species* published in 1869 included Spencer's phrase as an alternative to natural selection, with credit given: "But the expression often used by Mr. Herbert Spencer, of the Survival of the Fittest, is more accurate, and is sometimes equally convenient." Although the phrase is still often used by non-biologists, modern biologists avoid it because it is tautological if 'fittest' is read to mean 'functionally superior' and is applied to individuals rather than considered as an averaged quantity over populations.

Modern Evolutionary Synthesis

Natural selection relies crucially on the idea of heredity, but it was developed long before the basic concepts of genetics. Although the Austrian monk Gregor Mendel, the father of modern genetics, was a contemporary of Darwin's, his work would lie in obscurity until the early 20th century.

Only after the integration of Darwin's theory of evolution with a complex statistical appreciation of Gregor Mendel's 're-discovered' laws of inheritance did natural selection become generally accepted by scientists. The work of Ronald Fisher (who developed the required mathematical language and The Genetical Theory of Natural Selection), J.B.S. Haldane (who introduced the concept of the "cost" of natural selection), Sewall Wright (who elucidated the nature of selection and adaptation), Theodosius Dobzhansky (who established the idea that mutation, by creating genetic diversity, supplied the raw material for natural selection: see Genetics and the Origin of Species), William Hamilton (who conceived of kin selection), Ernst Mayr (who recognised the key importance of reproductive isolation for speciation: see Systematics and the Origin of Species) and many others formed the modern evolutionary synthesis. This synthesis cemented natural selection as the foundation of evolutionary theory, where it remains today.

Impact of the Idea

Darwin's ideas, along with those of Adam Smith and Karl Marx, had a profound influence on 19th century thought. Perhaps the most radical claim of the theory of evolution through natural selection is that "elaborately constructed forms, so different from each other, and dependent on each other in so complex a manner" evolved from the simplest forms of life by a few simple principles. This claim inspired some of Darwin's most ardent supporters—and provoked the most profound opposition. The radicalism of natural selection, according to Stephen Jay Gould, lay in its power to "dethrone some of the deepest and most traditional comforts of Western thought". In particular, it challenged long-standing beliefs in such concepts as a special and exalted place for humans in the natural world and a benevolent creator whose intentions were reflected in nature's order and design.

Cell and Molecular Biology

In the 19th century, Wilhelm Roux, a founder of modern embryology, wrote a book entitled *'Der Kampf der Teile im Organismus'* (The struggle of parts in the organism) in which he suggested that the development of an organism results from a Darwinian competition between the parts of the embryo, occurring at all levels, from molecules to organs. In recent years, a modern version of this theory has been proposed by Jean-Jacques Kupiec. According to this cellular Darwinism, stochasticity at the molecular level generates diversity in cell types whereas cell interactions impose a characteristic order on the developing embryo.

Social and Psychological Theory

The social implications of the theory of evolution by natural selection also became the source of continuing controversy. Friedrich Engels, a German political philosopher and co-originator of the ideology of communism, wrote in 1872 that "Darwin did not know what a bitter satire he wrote on mankind when he showed that free competition, the struggle for existence, which the economists celebrate as the highest historical achievement, is the normal state of the animal kingdom". Interpretation of natural selection as necessarily 'progressive', leading to increasing 'advances' in intelligence and civilisation, was used as a justification for colonialism and policies of eugenics, as well as broader sociopolitical positions now described as Social Darwinism. Konrad Lorenz won the Nobel Prize in Physiology or Medicine in 1973 for his analysis of animal behaviour in terms of the role of natural selection (particularly group selection). However, in Germany in 1940, in writings that he subsequently disowned, he used the theory as a justification for policies of the Nazi state. He wrote ". . . selection for toughness, heroism, and social utility. . . must be accomplished by some human institution, if mankind, in default of selective factors, is not to be ruined by domestication-induced degeneracy. The racial idea as the basis of our state has already accomplished much in this respect."

Others have developed ideas that human societies and culture evolve by mechanisms that are analogous to those that apply to evolution of species.

More recently, work among anthropologists and psychologists has led to the development of sociobiology and later evolutionary psychology, a field that attempts to explain features of human psychology in terms of adaptation to the ancestral environment. The most prominent such example, notably advanced in the early work of Noam Chomsky and later by Steven Pinker, is the hypothesis that the human brain is adapted to acquire the grammatical rules of natural language. Other aspects of human behaviour and social structures, from specific cultural norms such as incest avoidance to broader patterns such as gender roles, have been hypothesized to have similar origins as adaptations to the early environment in which modern humans evolved. By analogy to the action of natural selection on genes, the concept of memes — "units of cultural transmission", or culture's equivalents of genes undergoing selection and recombination — has arisen, first described in this form by Richard Dawkins and subsequently expanded upon by philosophers such as Daniel Dennett as explanations for complex cultural activities, including human consciousness. Extensions of the theory of natural selection to such a wide range of cultural phenomena have been distinctly controversial and are not widely accepted.

Information and Systems Theory

In 1922, Alfred Lotka proposed that natural selection might be understood as a physical principle which could be described in terms of the use of energy by a system, a concept that was later developed by Howard Odum as the maximum power principle whereby evolutionary systems with selective advantage maximise the rate of useful energy transformation. Such concepts are sometimes relevant in the study of applied thermodynamics.

The principles of natural selection have inspired a variety of computational techniques, such as 'soft' artificial life, that simulate selective processes and can be highly efficient in 'adapting' entities to an environment defined by a specified fitness function. For example, a class of heuristic optimization algorithms known as genetic algorithms, pioneered by John Holland in the 1970s and expanded upon by David E. Goldberg, identify optimal solutions by simulated reproduction and mutation of a population of solutions defined by an initial probability distribution. Such algorithms are particularly useful when applied to problems whose solution landscape is very rough or has many local minima.

Genetic Basis of Natural Selection

The idea of natural selection predates the understanding of genetics. We now have a much better idea of the biology underlying heritability, which is the basis of natural selection.

Genotype and Phenotype

Natural selection acts on an organism's phenotype, or physical characteristics. Phenotype is determined by an organism's genetic make-up (genotype) and the environment in which the organism lives. Often, natural selection acts on specific traits of an individual, and the terms phenotype and genotype are used narrowly to indicate these specific traits.

When different organisms in a population possess different versions of a gene for a certain trait, each of these versions is known as an allele. It is this genetic variation that underlies phenotypic traits. A typical example is that certain combinations of genes for eye colour in humans which, for instance, give rise to the phenotype of blue eyes. (On the other hand, when all the organisms in a population share the same allele for a particular trait, and this state is stable over time, the allele is said to be *fixed* in that population.)

Some traits are governed by only a single gene, but most traits are influenced by the interactions of many genes. A variation in one of the many genes that contributes to a trait may have only a small effect on the phenotype; together, these genes can produce a continuum of possible phenotypic values.

Directionality of Selection

When some component of a trait is heritable, selection will alter the frequencies of the different alleles, or variants of the gene that produces the variants of the trait. Selection can be divided into three classes, on the basis of its effect on allele frequencies:

Directional selection occurs when a certain allele has a greater fitness than others, resulting in an increase of its frequency. This process can continue until the allele is fixed and the entire population shares the fitter phenotype. It is directional selection that is illustrated in the antibiotic resistance example above.

Far more common is stabilizing selection (which is commonly confused with *'purifying selection'*, which lowers the frequency of alleles that have a deleterious effect on the phenotype — that is, produce organisms of lower fitness. This process can continue until the allele is eliminated from the population. Purifying selection results in functional genetic features, such as protein-coding genes or regulatory sequences, being conserved over time due to selective pressure against deleterious variants.

Finally, a number of forms of *balancing selection* exist, which do not result in fixation, but maintain an allele at intermediate frequencies in a population. This can occur in diploid species (that is, those that have two pairs of chromosomes) when heterozygote individuals, who have different alleles on each chromosome at a single genetic locus, have a higher fitness than homozygote individuals that have two of the same alleles. This is called heterozygote advantage or overdominance, of which the best-known example is the malarial resistance observed in heterozygous humans who carry only one copy of the gene for sickle cell anaemia.

Maintenance of allelic variation can also occur through disruptive or diversifying selection, which favors genotypes that depart from the average in either direction (that is, the opposite of overdominance), and can result in a bimodal distribution of trait values. Finally, balancing selection can occur through frequency-dependent selection, where the fitness of one particular phenotype depends on the distribution of other phenotypes in the population. The principles of game theory have been applied to understand the fitness distributions in these situations, particularly in the study of kin selection and the evolution of reciprocal altruism.

Genetic Linkage

Genetic linkage occurs when the loci of two alleles are *linked*, or in close proximity to each other on the chromosome. During the formation of gametes, recombination of the genetic material results in reshuffling of the alleles. However, the chance that such a reshuffle occurs between two alleles depends on the distance between those alleles; the closer the alleles are to each other, the less likely it is that such a reshuffle will occur. Consequently, when selection targets one allele, this automatically results in selection of the other allele as well; through this mechanism, selection can have a strong influence on patterns of variation in the genome.

Selective sweeps occur when an allele becomes more common in a population as a result of positive selection. As the prevalence of one allele increases, linked alleles can also become more common, whether they are neutral or even slightly deleterious. This is called *genetic hitchhiking*. A strong selective sweep results in a region of the genome where the positively selected haplotype (the allele and its neighbours) are essentially the only ones that exist in the population.

Whether a selective sweep has occurred or not can be investigated by measuring linkage disequilibrium, or whether a given haplotype is overrepresented in the population. Normally, genetic recombination results in a reshuffling of the different alleles within a haplotype, and none of the haplotypes will dominate the population. However, during a selective sweep, selection for a specific allele will also result in selection of neighbouring alleles. Therefore, the presence of a block of strong linkage disequilibrium might indicate that there has been a 'recent' selective sweep near the centre of the block, and this can be used to identify sites recently under selection. Background selection is the opposite of a selective sweep. If a specific site experiences strong and persistent purifying selection, linked variation will tend to be weeded out along with it, producing a region in the genome of low overall variability. Because background selection is a result of deleterious new mutations, which can occur randomly in any haplotype, it does not produce clear blocks of linkage disequilibrium, although with low recombination it can still lead to slightly negative linkage disequilibrium overall.

Genome Project

Genome projects are scientific endeavours that ultimately aim to determine the complete genome sequence of an organism (be it an animal, a plant, a fungus, a bacterium, an archaean, a protist or a virus). The genome sequence for any organism requires the DNA sequences for each of the chromosomes in an organism to be determined. For bacteria, which usually have just one chromosome, a genome project will aim to map the sequence of that chromosome. Humans, with 22 pairs of autosomes and 2 sex chromosomes, will require 46 separate chromosome sequences in order to represent the completed genome.

The Human Genome Project was a landmark genome project that is already having a major impact on research across the life sciences, with potential for spurring numerous medical and commercial developments.

Genome assembly refers to the process of taking a large number of short DNA sequences, all of which were generated by a shotgun sequencing project, and putting them back together to create a representation of the original chromosomes from which the DNA originated. In a shotgun sequencing project, all the DNA from a source (usually a single organism, anything from a bacterium to a mammal) is first fractured into millions of small pieces. These pieces are then 'read' by automated sequencing machines, which can read up to 900 nucleotides or bases at a time. (The four bases are adenine, guanine, cytosine, and thymine, represented as AGCT.) A genome assembly algorithm works by taking all the pieces and aligning them to one another, and detecting all places where two of the short sequences, or *reads*, overlap. These overlapping reads can be merged together, and the process continues.

Genome assembly is a very difficult computational problem, made more difficult because many genomes contain large numbers of identical sequences, known as *repeats*. These repeats can be thousands of nucleotides long, and some occur in thousands of different locations, especially in the large genomes of plants and animals.

The resulting (draft) genome sequence is produced by combining the information sequenced contigs and then employing linking information to create scaffolds. Scaffolds are positioned along the physical map of the chromosomes creating a 'golden path'.

Assembly Software

Originally, most large-scale DNA sequencing centers developed their own software for assembling the sequences that they produced. However, this has changed as the software has grown more complex and as the number of sequencing centres has increased. An example of such assembler *Short Oligonucleotide Analysis Package* developed by BGI for de novo assembly of human-sized genomes, alignment, SNP detection, resequencing, indel finding, and structural variation analysis.

Genome Annotation

Genome annotation is the process of attaching biological information to sequences. It consists of two main steps:

- identifying elements on the genome, a process called gene prediction; and
- attaching biological information to these elements.

Automatic annotation tools try to perform all this by computer analysis, as opposed to manual annotation (a.k.a. curation) which involves human expertise. Ideally, these approaches co-exist and complement each other in the same annotation pipeline.

The basic level of annotation is using BLAST for finding similarities, and then annotating genomes based on that. However, nowadays more and more additional information is added to the annotation platform. The additional information allows manual annotators to deconvolute discrepancies between genes that are given the same annotation. Some databases use genome context information, similarity scores, experimental data, and integrations of other resources to provide genome annotations through their Subsystems approach. Other databases (e.g Ensembl) rely on both curated data sources as well as a range of different software tools in their automated genome annotation pipeline.

Structural annotation consists of the identification of genomic elements.

- ORFs and their localisation
- gene structure
- coding regions
- location of regulatory motifs

Functional annotation consists of attaching biological information to genomic elements.

- biochemical function
- biological function
- involved regulation and interactions
- expression

These steps may involve both biological experiments and *in silico* analysis.

A variety of software tools have been developed to permit scientists to view and share genome annotations.

Genome annotation is the next major challenge for the Human Genome Project, now that the genome sequences of human and several model organisms are largely complete. Identifying the locations of genes and other genetic control elements is often described as defining the biological 'parts list' for the assembly and normal operation of an organism. Scientists are still at an early stage in the process of delineating this parts list and in understanding how all the parts 'fit together'.

Genome annotation is an active area of investigation and involves a number of different organizations in the life science community which publish the results of their efforts in publicly available biological databases accessible via the web and other electronic means. Here is an alphabetical listing of on-going projects relevant to genome annotation:

- Encyclopedia of DNA Elements (ENCODE)
- Entrez Gene
- Ensembl
- Gene ontology consortium
- GeneRIF
- RefSeq
- Uniprot
- Vertebrate and Genome Annotation Project (Vega)

At Wikipedia, genome annotation has started to become automated under the auspices of the Gene Wiki portal which operates a bot that harvests gene data from research databases and creates gene stubs on that basis.

When is a Genome Project Finished?

When sequencing a genome, there are usually regions that are difficult to sequence (often regions with highly repetitive DNA). Thus, 'completed' genome sequences are rarely ever complete, and terms such as 'working draft' or 'essentially complete' have been used to more accurately describe the status of such genome projects. Even when every base pair of a genome sequence has been determined, there are still likely to be errors present because DNA sequencing is not a completely accurate process. It could also be argued that a complete genome project should include the sequences of mitochondria and (for plants) chloroplasts as these organelles have their own genomes.

It is often reported that the goal of sequencing a genome is to obtain information about the complete set of genes in that particular genome sequence. The proportion of a genome that encodes for genes may be very small (particularly in eukaryotes such as humans, where coding DNA may only account for a few per cent of the entire sequence). However, it is not always possible (or desirable) to only sequence the coding regions separately. Also, as scientists understand more about the role of this noncoding DNA (often referred to as junk DNA), it will become more important to have a complete genome sequence as a background to understanding the genetics and biology of any given organism.

In many ways genome projects do not confine themselves to only determining a DNA sequence of an organism. Such projects may also include gene prediction to find out where the genes are in a genome, and what those genes do. There may also be related projects to sequence ESTs or mRNAs to help find out where the genes actually are.

Historical and Technological Perspectives

Historically, when sequencing eukaryotic genomes (such as the worm *Caenorhabditis elegans*) it was common to first map the genome to provide a series of landmarks across the genome. Rather than sequence a chromosome in one go, it would be sequenced piece by piece (with the prior knowledge of approximately where that piece is located on the larger chromosome). Changes in technology and in particular improvements to the processing power of computers, means that genomes can now be 'shotgun sequenced' in one go (there are caveats to this approach though when compared to the traditional approach).

Improvements in DNA sequencing technology has meant that the cost of sequencing a new genome sequence has steadily fallen (in terms of cost per base pair) and newer technology has also meant that genomes can be sequenced far more quickly. When research agencies decide what new genomes to sequence, the emphasis has been on species which have either a relevance to human health (e.g. pathogenic bacteria or vectors of disease such as mosquitos) or species which have commercial importance (e.g. livestock and crop plants). Secondary emphasis is placed on species whose genomes will help answer important questions in molecular evolution (e.g. the common chimpanzee).

In the future, it is likely that it will become even cheaper and quicker to sequence a genome. This will allow for complete genome sequences to be determined from many different individuals of the same species. For humans, this will allow us to better understand aspects of human genetic diversity.

Heredity

Heredity is the passing of traits to offspring (from its parent or ancestors). This is the process by which an offspring cell or organism acquires or becomes predisposed to the characteristics of its parent cell or organism. Through heredity, variations exhibited by individuals can accumulate and cause a species to evolve. The study of heredity in biology is called genetics, which includes the field of epigenetics.

The ancients had a variety of ideas about heredity: Theophrastus proposed that male flowers caused female flowers to ripen; Hippocrates speculated that 'seeds' were produced by various body parts and transmitted to offspring at the time of conception, and Aristotle thought that male and female semen mixed at conception. Aeschylus, in 458 BC, proposed the male as the parent, with the female as a 'nurse for the young life sown within her'.

Various hereditary mechanisms were envisaged without being properly tested or quantified. These included blending inheritance and the inheritance of acquired traits. Nevertheless, people were able to develop domestic breeds of animals as well as crops through artificial selection. The inheritance of acquired traits also formed a part of early Lamarckian ideas on evolution.

In the 9th century AD, the Afro-Arab writer Al-Jahiz considered the effects of the environment on the likelihood of an animal to survive, and first described the struggle for existence. His ideas on the struggle for existence in the *Book of Animals* have been summarized as follows:

> "Animals engage in a struggle for existence; for resources, to avoid being eaten and to breed. Environmental factors influence organisms to develop new characteristics to ensure survival, thus transforming into new species. Animals that survive to breed can pass on their successful characteristics to offspring".

In 1000 AD, the Arab physician, Abu al-Qasim al-Zahrawi (known as Albucasis in the West), wrote the first clear description of haemophilia, a hereditary genetic disorder, in his *Al-Tasrif*. In this work, he wrote of an Andalusian family whose males died of bleeding after minor injuries.

During the 18th century, Dutch microscopist Antonie van Leeuwenhoek (1632-1723) discovered 'animalcules' in the sperm of humans and other animals. Some scientists speculated they saw a 'little man' (homunculus) inside each sperm. These scientists formed a school of thought known as the 'spermists'. They contended the only contributions of the female to the next generation were the womb in which the homunculus grew, and prenatal influences of the womb. An opposing school of thought, the ovists, believed that the future human was in the egg, and that sperm merely stimulated the growth of the egg. Ovists thought women carried eggs containing boy and girl children, and that the gender of the offspring was determined well before conception.

Pangenesis was an idea that males and females formed 'pangenes' in every organ. These pangenes subsequently moved through their blood to the genitals and then to the children. The concept originated with the ancient Greeks, and influenced biology until as recently as a century ago.

The terms 'blood relative', 'bloodline', 'full-blooded', and 'royal blood' are relics of pangenesis. Francis Galton, Charles Darwin's cousin, experimentally tested and disproved pangenesis during the 1870s.

TYPES OF HEREDITY

Dominant and Recessive

An allele is said to be dominant if it is always expressed in the appearance of an organism (phenotype). For example, in peas the allele for green pods, *G*, is dominant to that for yellow pods, *g*. Since the allele for green pods is dominant, pea plants with the pair of alleles *GG* (homozygote) or *Gg* (heterozygote) will have green pods. The allele for yellow pods is recessive. The effects of this allele are only seen when it is present in both chromosomes, *gg* (homozygote).

The description of a mode of biological inheritance consists of three main categories:

1. **Number of involved loci**
   - Monogenetic (also called 'simple') – one locus
   - Oligogenetic – few loci
   - Polygenetic – many loci
2. **Involved chromosomes**
   - Autosomal – loci are not situated on a sex chromosome
   - Gonosomal – loci are situated on a sex chromosome
   - *X*-chromosomal – loci are situated on the *X* chromo-some (the more common case)
   - *Y*-chromosomal – loci are situated on the *Y* chromosome
   - Mitochondrial – loci are situated on the mitochondrial DNA

3. **Correlation genotype–phenotype**
   - Dominant
   - Intermediate (also called 'codominant')
   - Recessive

These three categories are part of every exact description of a mode of inheritance in the above order. Additionally, more specifications may be added as follows:

4. **Coincidental and environmental interactions**
   - Penetrance
   - Complete
   - Incomplete (percentual number)
   - Expressivity
   - Invariable
   - Variable
   - Heritability (in polygenetic and sometimes also in oligogenetic modes of inheritance)
   - Maternal or paternal imprinting phenomena
5. **Sex-linked interactions**
   - Sex-linked inheritance (gonosomal loci)
   - Sex-limited phenotype expression (e.g., cryptorchism)
   - Inheritance through the maternal line (in case of mitochondrial DNA loci)
   - Inheritance through the paternal line (in case of *Y*-chromosomal loci)
6. **Locus-locus interactions**
   - Epistasis with other loci (e.g., overdominance)
   - Gene coupling with other loci
   - Homozygotous lethal factors
   - Semi-lethal factors

Determination and description of a mode of inheritance is primarily achieved through statistical analysis of pedigree data. In case the involved loci are known, methods of molecular genetics can also be employed.

When Charles Darwin proposed his theory of evolution in 1859, one of its major problems was the lack of an underlying mechanism for heredity. Darwin believed in a mix of blending inheritance and the inheritance of acquired traits (pangenesis). Blending inheritance would lead to uniformity across populations in only a few generations and thus would remove variation from a population on which natural selection could act. This led to Darwin adopting some Lamarckian ideas in later editions of *On the Origin of Species* and his later biological works. Darwin's primary approach to heredity was to outline how it appeared to work (noticing that traits could be inherited which were not expressed explicitly in the parent at the time of reproduction, that certain traits could be sex-linked, etc.) rather than suggesting mechanisms.

Darwin's initial model of heredity was adopted by, and then heavily modified by, his cousin Francis Galton, who laid the framework for the biometric school of heredity. Galton rejected the aspects of Darwin's pangenesis model which relied on acquired traits.

The inheritance of acquired traits was shown to have little basis in the 1880s when August Weismann cut the tails off many generations of mice and found that their offspring continued to develop tails.

Gregor Mendel — Father of Modern Genetics

The idea of particulate inheritance of genes can be attributed to the Moravian monk Gregor Mendel who published his work on pea plants in 1865. However, his work was not widely known and was rediscovered in 1901. It was initially assumed the Mendelian inheritance only accounted for large (qualitative) differences, such as those seen by

Mendel in his pea plants—and the idea of additive effect of (quantitative) genes was not realised until R.A. Fisher's (1918) paper, "The Correlation Between Relatives on the Supposition of Mendelian Inheritance".

Modern Development of Genetics and Heredity

In the 1930s, work by Fisher and others resulted in a combination of Mendelian and biometric schools into the modern evolutionary synthesis. The modern synthesis bridged the gap between experimental geneticists and naturalists; and between both and palaeontologists, stating that:

> 'All evolutionary phenomena can be explained in a way consistent with known genetic mechanisms and the observational evidence of naturalists'.

Evolution is gradual: small genetic changes, recombination ordered by natural selection. Discontinuities amongst species (or other taxa) are explained as originating gradually through geographical separation and extinction (not saltation).

Selection is overwhelmingly the main mechanism of change; even slight advantages are important when continued. The object of selection is the phenotype in its surrounding environment. The role of genetic drift is equivocal; though strongly supported initially by Dobzhansky, it was downgraded later as results from ecological genetics were obtained.

The primacy of population thinking: the genetic diversity carried in natural populations is a key factor in evolution. The strength of natural selection in the wild was greater than expected; the effect of ecological factors such as niche occupation and the significance of barriers to gene flow are all important.

In palaeontology, the ability to explain historical observations by extrapolation from micro to macro-evolution is proposed. Historical contingency means explanations at different levels may exist. Gradualism does not mean constant rate of change.

The idea that speciation occurs after populations are reproductively isolated has been much debated. In plants, polyploidy must be included in any view of speciation. Formulations such as 'evolution consists primarily of changes in the frequencies of alleles between one generation and another' were proposed rather later. The traditional view is that developmental biology ('evo-devo') played little part in the synthesis, but an account of Gavin de Beer's work by Stephen Jay Gould suggests he may be an exception.

Almost all aspects of the synthesis have been challenged at times, with varying degrees of success. There is no doubt, however, that the synthesis was a great landmark in evolutionary biology. It cleared up many confusions, and was directly responsible for stimulating a great deal of research in the post-World War II era.

Heritability

Heritability is the proportion of phenotypic variation in a population that is attributable to genetic variation among individuals. Phenotypic variation among individuals may be due to genetic and/or environmental factors. Heritability analyses estimate the relative contributions of differences in genetic and non-genetic factors to the total phenotypic variance in a population. Often measured empirically, heritability is an important notion in quantitative genetics, particularly in selective breeding, but less so in the general theory of population genetics.

Pay close attention to the variation part of 'phenotypic variation': if a trait has a heritability of 0.5, it means that the phenotypic variation is 50 per cent due to genetic variation. It does not imply that the trait is 50 per cent caused by genetics.

Heritability is specific to a particular population in a particular environment, but the extent of the dependence on environment is also a function of the genes involved. Individuals with the same genotype can exhibit different phenotypes through a mechanism called phenotypic plasticity, which makes their heritability difficult to measure in some cases. Recent insights in molecular biology have identified changes in transcriptional activity of individual genes associated with environmental changes. However, there are a large number of genes whose transcription is not affected by the environment.

Rather than look at all the traits of an organism, heritability focuses on the differences between multiple organisms for a single trait. Because heritability is concerned with variance, it is necessarily a description of a certain population — not an individual.

A population of asians would contain individuals with genetics that code only for black hair. In this case, heritability is of course 0, since there is no variance in hair colour to analyse. But suppose some individuals dyed their hair and increased the population's variance in hair colours. Although now there are some differences in hair colour, theoretically heritability would still be 0 (i.e. 0% of the variance is due to differences in genetics).

Oppositely, imagine a population of mixed races where hair dye is forbidden. Now there is again variance in hair colour, but this time heritability is 1 (i.e. 100% of the variance is due to differences in genetics). Of course, that would be assuming that our population's hair colours truly have *nothing* to do with environmental factors (like amount of sunlight). In practice, heritability is not that simple; environment and genetics interact.

Estimating Heritability

Estimating heritability is not a simple process, since only P can be observed or measured directly. Measuring the genetic and environmental variance requires various sophisticated statistical methods. These methods give better estimates when using data from closely related individuals — such as brothers, sisters, parents and offspring, rather than from more distantly related ones. The standard error for heritability estimates is generally very poor unless the dataset is large.

In non-human populations it is often possible to collect information in a controlled way. For example, among farm animals it is easy to arrange for a bull to produce offspring from a large number of cows. Due to ethical concerns, such a degree of experimental control is impossible when gathering human data.

As a result, studies of human heritability sometimes contrast identical twins who have been separated early in life and raised in different environments. Such individuals have identical genotypes and can be used to separate the effects of genotype and environment.

Twin studies entail problems of their own, such as: independently raised twins shared a common prenatal environment; they may have undergone intrauterine competition; the mother may be more physically stressed (less nutrients); and twins reared apart are difficult to find, and may reflect certain types of environments.

Heritability estimates are always relative to the genetic and environmental factors in the population, and are not absolute measurements of the contribution of genetic and environmental factors to a phenotype. Heritability estimates reflect the amount of variation in genotypic effects compared to variation in environmental effects.

Heritability can be made larger by diversifying the genetic background, e.g., by using only very outbred individuals (which increases the Variance(G)) and/or by minimizing environmental effects (which decreases the Variance(E)). Smaller heritability, on the other hand, can be generated by using inbred individuals (which decreases the

Variance(*G*)) or individuals reared in very diverse environments (which increases the Variance(*E*)). Due to such effects, different populations of a species might have different heritabilities even for the same trait.

In observational studies *G* and *E* may be correlated, giving rise to gene environment correlation. Depending on the methods used to estimate heritability, correlations between genetic factors and shared or non-shared environments may or may not be included in the total heritability estimate.

Because of the contextual nature of measured heritabilities, paradoxes often arise. For example, the heritability of a trait could be near 100 per cent in one study and close to zero in another. In one study, e.g., a group of unrelated army recruits may be given identical training and nutrition and then their muscular strength may be measured.

The variation in strength observed after the (identical) training will translate into a high heritability estimate. In another study, whose purpose might be to assess the efficacy of various workout regimes or nutritional programmes, study subjects may be first chosen to match each other as closely as possible in prior physical characteristics before some of them are put onto Programme *A* and others onto Programme *B*, and this will lead to a low heritability estimate.

Heritability estimates are often misinterpreted. Heritability refers to the proportion of variation between individuals in a population that is influenced by genetic factors. Heritability describes the population, not individuals within that population. For example, It is incorrect to say that since the heritability of a personality trait is about .6, that means that 60 per cent of your personality is inherited from your parents and 40 per cent comes from the environment.

The heritability estimate changes according to the genetic and environmental variability present in the population. In studies of genetically identical inbred animals, all traits have zero heritability. Heritability estimates can be much higher in outbred (genetically variable) populations under very homogeneous environments.

A highly genetically loaded trait (such as eye colour) still assumes environmental input within normal limits (a certain range of temperature, oxygen in the atmosphere, etc.). A more useful distinction than "nature *vs*. nurture" is "obligate *vs*. facultative" – under typical environmental ranges, what traits are more 'obligate' (e.g., the nose—everyone has a nose) or more 'facultative' (sensitive to environmental variations, such as specific language learned during infancy). Another useful distinction is between traits that are likely to be adaptations (such as the nose) *vs*. those that are byproducts of adaptations (such the white colour of bones), or are due to random variation (non-adaptive variation in, say, nose shape or size).

Larger Models

When a large, complex pedigree is available for estimating heritability, the most efficient use of the data is in a restricted maximum likelihood (REML) model. The raw data will usually have three or more datapoints for each individual: a code for the sire, a code for the dam and one or several trait values. Different trait values may be for different traits or for different timepoints of measurement.

The currently popular methodology relies on high degrees of certainty over the identities of the sire and dam; it is not common to treat the sire identity probabilistically. This is not usually a problem, since the methodology is rarely applied to wild populations (although it has been used for several wild ungulate and bird populations), and sires are invariably known with a very high degree of certainty in breeding programmes. There are also algorithms that account for uncertain paternity.

The pedigrees can be viewed using programmes such as Pedigree Viewer , and analysed with programmes such as ASReml, VCE , WOMBAT or BLUPF90 family's programmes.

Response to Selection

In selective breeding of plants and animals, the expected response to selection can be estimated by the following equation:

$$R = h^2S$$

In this equation, the Response to Selection (R) is defined as the realized average difference between the parent generation and the next generation. The Selection Differential (S) is defined as the average difference between the parent generation and the selected parents.

For example, imagine that a plant breeder is involved in a selective breeding project with the aim of increasing the number of kernels per ear of corn. For the sake of argument, let us assume that the average ear of corn in the parent generation has 100 kernels. Let us also assume that the selected parents produce corn with an average of 120 kernels per ear. If h^2 equals 0.5, then the next generation will produce corn with an average of 0.5(120-100) = 10 additional kernels per ear. Therefore, the total number of kernels per ear of corn will equal, on average, 110.

Ribonucleic Acid

Ribonucleic acid (*RNA*) is a biologically important type of molecule that consists of a long chain of nucleotide units. Each nucleotide consists of a nitrogenous base, a ribose sugar, and a phosphate. RNA is very similar to DNA, but differs in a few important structural details: in the cell, RNA is usually single-stranded, while DNA is usually double-stranded; RNA nucleotides contain ribose while DNA contains deoxyribose (a type of ribose that lacks one oxygen atom); and RNA has the base uracil rather than thymine that is present in DNA. RNA is transcribed from DNA by enzymes called RNA polymerases and is generally further processed by other enzymes. RNA is central to protein synthesis. Here, a type of RNA called messenger RNA carries information from DNA to structures called ribosomes. These ribosomes are made from proteins and ribosomal RNAs, which come together to form a molecular machine that can read messenger RNAs and translate the information they carry into proteins. There are many RNAs with other roles — in particular regulating which genes are expressed, but also as the genomes of most viruses.

RNA and DNA are both nucleic acids, but differ in three main ways. First, unlike DNA which is double-stranded, RNA is a single-stranded molecule in most of its biological roles and has a much shorter chain of nucleotides. Second, while DNA contains *deoxyribose,* RNA contains *ribose* (there is no hydroxyl group attached to the pentose ring in the 2' position in DNA). These hydroxyl groups make RNA less stable than DNA because it is more prone to hydrolysis. Third, the complementary base to adenine is not thymine, as it is in DNA, but rather uracil, which is an unmethylated form of thymine.

Like DNA, most biologically active RNAs, including mRNA, tRNA, rRNA, snRNAs and other non-coding RNAs, contain self-complementary sequences that allow parts of the RNA to fold and pair with itself to form double helices. Structural analysis of these RNAs has revealed that they are highly structured. Unlike DNA, their structures do not consist of long double helices but rather collections of short helices packed together into structures akin to proteins. In this fashion, RNAs can achieve chemical catalysis, like enzymes. For instance, determination of the structure of the ribosome—an enzyme that catalyzes peptide bond formation—revealed that its active site is composed entirely of RNA.

Each nucleotide in RNA contains a ribose sugar, with carbons numbered 1′ through 5′. A base is attached to the 1′ position, generally adenine (*A*), cytosine (*C*), guanine (*G*) or uracil (*U*). Adenine and guanine are purines, cytosine and uracil are pyrimidines. A phosphate group is attached to the 3′ position of one ribose and the 5′ position of the next. The phosphate groups have a negative charge each at physiological pH, making RNA a charged molecule (polyanion). The bases may form hydrogen bonds between cytosine and guanine, between adenine and uracil and between guanine and uracil. However other interactions are possible, such as a group of adenine bases binding to each other in a bulge, or the GNRA tetraloop that has a guanine–adenine base-pair.

An important structural feature of RNA that distinguishes it from DNA is the presence of a hydroxyl group at the 2' position of the ribose sugar. The presence of this functional group causes the helix to adopt the A-form geometry rather than the B-form most commonly observed in DNA. This results in a very deep and narrow major groove and a shallow and wide minor groove. A second consequence of the presence of the 2'-hydroxyl group is that in conformationally flexible regions of an RNA molecule (that is, not involved in formation of a double helix), it can chemically attack. RNA is transcribed with only four bases (adenine, cytosine, guanine and uracil), but there are numerous modified bases and sugars in mature RNAs. Pseudouridine (?), in which the linkage between uracil and ribose is changed from a C–N bond to a C-C bond, and ribothymidine (T), are found in various places (most notably in the T?C loop of tRNA). Another notable modified base is hypoxanthine, a deaminated adenine base whose nucleoside is called inosine (I). Inosine plays a key role in the wobble hypothesis of the genetic code. There are nearly 100 other naturally occurring modified nucleosides, of which pseudouridine and nucleosides with 2'-O-methylribose are the most common. The specific roles of many of these modifications in RNA are not fully understood. However, it is notable that in ribosomal RNA, many of the post-transcriptional modifications occur in highly functional regions, such as the peptidyl transferase centre and the subunit interface, implying that they are important for normal function.

The functional form of single stranded RNA molecules, just like proteins, frequently requires a specific tertiary structure. The scaffold for this structure is provided by secondary structural elements which are hydrogen bonds within the molecule. This leads to several recognizable 'domains' of secondary structure like hairpin loops, bulges and internal loops. Since RNA is charged, metal ions such as Mg^{2+} are needed to stabilise many secondary and tertiary structures.

Synthesis

Synthesis of RNA is usually catalyzed by an enzyme–RNA polymerase—using DNA as a template, a process known as transcription. Initiation of transcription begins with the binding of the enzyme to a promoter sequence in the DNA (usually found 'upstream' of a gene). The DNA double helix is unwound by the helicase activity of the enzyme. The enzyme then progresses along the template strand in the 3′ to 5′ direction, synthesizing a complementary RNA molecule with elongation occurring in the 5′ to 3′ direction. The DNA sequence also dictates where termination of RNA synthesis will occur.

RNAs are often modified by enzymes after transcription. For example, a poly(A) tail and a 5' cap are added to eukaryotic pre-mRNA and introns are removed by the spliceosome.

There are also a number of RNA-dependent RNA polymerases that use RNA as their template for synthesis of a new strand of RNA. For instance, a number of RNA viruses (such as poliovirus) use this type of enzyme to replicate their genetic material. Also, RNA-dependent RNA polymerase is part of the RNA interference pathway in many organisms.

Messenger RNA (mRNA) is the RNA that carries information from DNA to the ribosome, the sites of protein synthesis (translation) in the cell. The coding sequence of the mRNA determines the amino acid sequence in the protein that is produced. Many RNAs do not code for protein however (about 97% of the transcriptional output is non-protein-coding in eukaryotes.

These so-called non-coding RNAs ("ncRNA") can be encoded by their own genes (RNA genes), but can also derive from mRNA introns. The most prominent examples of non-coding RNAs are transfer RNA (tRNA) and ribosomal RNA (rRNA), both of which are involved in the process of translation. There are also non-coding RNAs involved in gene regulation, RNA processing and other roles. Certain RNAs are able to catalyse chemical reactions such as cutting and ligating other RNA molecules, and the catalysis of peptide bond formation in the ribosome; these are known as ribozymes.

In Translation

Messenger RNA (mRNA) carries information about a protein sequence to the ribosomes, the protein synthesis factories in the cell. It is coded so that every three nucleotides (a codon) correspond to one amino acid. In eukaryotic cells, once precursor mRNA (pre-mRNA) has been transcribed from DNA, it is processed to mature mRNA. This removes its introns–non-coding sections of the pre-mRNA. The mRNA is then exported from the nucleus to the cytoplasm, where it is bound to ribosomes and translated into its corresponding protein form with the help of tRNA. In prokaryotic cells, which do not have nucleus and cytoplasm compartments, mRNA can bind to ribosomes while it is being transcribed from DNA. After a certain amount of time the message degrades into its component nucleotides with the assistance of ribonucleases.

Transfer RNA (tRNA) is a small RNA chain of about 80 nucleotides that transfers a specific amino acid to a growing polypeptide chain at the ribosomal site of protein synthesis during translation. It has sites for amino acid attachment and an anticodon region for codon recognition that binds to a specific sequence on the messenger RNA chain through hydrogen bonding.

Ribosomal RNA (rRNA) is the catalytic component of the ribosomes. Eukaryotic ribosomes contain four different rRNA molecules: 18S, 5.8S, 28S and 5S rRNA. Three of the rRNA molecules are synthesized in the nucleolus, and one is synthesized elsewhere. In the cytoplasm, ribosomal RNA and protein combine to form a nucleoprotein called a ribosome. The ribosome binds mRNA and carries out protein synthesis. Several ribosomes may be attached to a single mRNA at any time. rRNA is extremely abundant and makes up 80 per cent of the 10 mg/ml RNA found in a typical eukaryotic cytoplasm.

Transfer-messenger RNA (tmRNA) is found in many bacteria and plastids. It tags proteins encoded by mRNAs that lack stop codons for degradation and prevents the ribosome from stalling.

Regulatory RNAs

Several types of RNA can downregulate gene expression by being complementary to a part of an mRNA or a gene's DNA. MicroRNAs (miRNA; 21-22 nt) are found in eukaryotes and act through RNA interference (RNAi), where an effector complex of miRNA and enzymes can break down mRNA which the miRNA is complementary to, block the mRNA from being translated, or accelerate its degradation. While small interfering RNAs (siRNA; 20-25 nt) are often produced by breakdown of viral RNA, there are also endogenous sources of siRNAs. siRNAs act through RNA interference in a fashion similar to miRNAs. Some miRNAs and siRNAs can cause genes they target to be methylated, thereby decreasing or increasing transcription of those genes. Animals have Piwi-interacting RNAs (piRNA; 29-30 nt) which are active in germline cells and are thought to be a defense against transposons and play a role in gametogenesis. Many prokaryotes have CRISPR RNAs, a regulatory system similar to RNA interference. Antisense RNAs are widespread; most downregulate a gene, but a few are activators of transcription. One way antisense RNA can act is by binding to an mRNA, forming double-stranded RNA that is enzymatically degraded. There are many long non-coding RNAs that regulate genes in eukaryotes, one such RNA is Xist which coats one X chromosome in female mammals and inactivates it.

An mRNA may contain regulatory elements itself, such as riboswitches, in the 5′ untranslated region or 3′

untranslated region; these cis-regulatory elements regulate the activity of that mRNA. The untranslated regions can also contain elements that regulate other genes. In RNA processing:

Many RNAs are involved in modifying other RNAs. Introns are spliced out of pre-mRNA by spliceosomes, which contain several small nuclear RNAs (snRNA), or the introns can be ribozymes that are spliced by themselves. RNA can also be altered by having its nucleotides modified to other nucleotides than *A, C, G* and *U*. In eukaryotes, modifications of RNA nucleotides are generally directed by small nucleolar RNAs (snoRNA; 60-300 nt), found in the nucleolus and cajal bodies. snoRNAs associate with enzymes and guide them to a spot on an RNA by basepairing to that RNA. These enzymes then perform the nucleotide modification. rRNAs and tRNAs are extensively modified, but snRNAs and mRNAs can also be the target of base modification.

RNA Genomes

Like DNA, RNA can carry genetic information. RNA viruses have genomes composed of RNA, and a variety of proteins encoded by that genome. The viral genome is replicated by some of those proteins, while other proteins protect the genome as the virus particle moves to a new host cell. Viroids are another group of pathogens, but they consist only of RNA, do not encode any protein and are replicated by a host plant cell's polymerase.

In Reverse Transcription

Reverse transcribing viruses replicate their genomes by reverse transcribing DNA copies from their RNA; these DNA copies are then transcribed to new RNA. Retrotransposons also spread by copying DNA and RNA from one another, and telomerase contains an RNA that is used as template for building the ends of eukaryotic chromosomes.

Double-stranded RNA

Double-stranded RNA (dsRNA) is RNA with two complementary strands, similar to the DNA found in all cells. dsRNA forms the genetic material of some viruses (double-stranded RNA viruses). Double-stranded RNA such as viral RNA or siRNA can trigger RNA interference in eukaryotes, as well as interferon response in vertebrates.

Nucleic acids were discovered in 1868 by Friedrich Miescher, who called the material 'nuclein' since it was found in the nucleus. It was later discovered that prokaryotic cells, which do not have a nucleus, also contain nucleic acids. The role of RNA in protein synthesis was suspected already in 1939. Severo Ochoa won the 1959 Nobel Prize in Medicine after he discovered how RNA is synthesized. The sequence of the 77 nucleotides of a yeast tRNA was found by Robert W. Holley in 1965, winning Holley the 1968 Nobel Prize in Medicine. In 1967, Carl Woese realized RNA can be catalytic and proposed that the earliest forms of life relied on RNA both to carry genetic information and to catalyze biochemical reactions—an RNA world. In 1976, Walter Fiers and his team determined the first complete nucleotide sequence of an RNA virus genome, that of bacteriophage MS2. In 1990 it was found in petunia that introduced genes can silence similar genes of the plant's own, now known to be a result of RNA interference. At about the same time, 22 nt long RNAs, now called microRNAs, were found to have a role in the development of *C. elegans*. The discovery of gene regulatory RNAs has led to attempts to develop drugs made of RNA, such as siRNA, to silence genes.

CHAPTER 13 Chromosomes in Humans

Chromosomes are thread like structures of DNA present in the cell nucleus, which are responsible for carrying genetic information. The word chromosome is derived from the Greek words for colour (*chroma*) and body (*soma*). In laboratory studies, chromosomes are stained easily with specific dyes, hence the name. Studying chromosomes in humans is an important aspect in genetics, as the phenotypic expression of an individual entirely depends on them. Also, genetic disorders are caused due to abnormalities in the chromosomes.

Chromosomes in Humans — An Overview

The human genome is diploid, meaning it contains 2 sets of chromosomes. As per researches in human genetics, it is found that more than 3 billion DNA base pairs are present in a single haploid human genome. In addition to these, chromosomes contain non-coding genes, regulatory elements and proteins. Together, they are arranged in an organized manner as chromosomes. Following are some points concerning facts about human chromosomes, which you may find interesting.

Number of Chromosomes in Humans

The total chromosomes can be expressed in diploid and haploid number. While the diploid number of chromosomes in humans is 46, the haploid number is 23. All normal human cells are diploid and the gametic cells (male gametes and female gametes) are haploid. In short, the number of chromosomes in humans differs, based on whether you are referring to a diploid cell or a haploid cell.

Sex Chromosomes in Humans

When we say sex chromosomes, they are used for determining the gender of an individual. Out of the 23 pairs of chromosomes, 22 are autosomal and 1 pair is the pair known as sex chromosomes. Males have one '*X*' and one '*Y*' chromosome, represented as (*XY*); whereas females have two copies of the same chromosome '*X*' (represented as *XX*). Besides humans, this *XY* sex-determination system is observed in many sexually reproducing organisms, like ginkgo biloba tree and Drosophila insect.

Chromosomes and Reproduction

In the process of fertilization, the male gamete that contains 22 autosomes and 1 sex chromosome (either *X* or *Y*) fuses with the female gamete that contains 22 autosomes and 1 sex chromosome (*X*) to form a diploid zygote. Thus, the resulting zygote has 44 autosomes and 2 sex chromosomes (may be *XX* or *XY*). Precisely speaking, two haploid cells or gametes fertilize to form a diploid cell during the reproduction process, thus retaining the typical chromosome number in humans.

Chromosome Abnormalities in Humans

Abnormalities in chromosomes are usually due to alterations in the chromosome number or structure. An example of genetic disorder due to extra chromosomes in humans is Down syndrome. In this condition, three copies of one chromosome is present in an individual, a condition known as trisomy. On the other hand, lack of one chromosome leads to an abnormality called monosomy. An example of this is Turner syndrome, a disease in females in which there is only one *X* chromosome.

Speaking about structural abnormalities of chromosomes in humans, they are caused either due to the presence of additional chromosomal parts (duplication) or lack of the same (deletion). In some conditions, sections of the chromosomes get exchanged between two chromosomes during cell division (translocation), resulting in a structural abnormality. In majority of the cases, abnormalities in the chromosomes of an offspring are inherited from its biological parents.

On a concluding note, presence of typical number of chromosomes in humans is imperative to express normal phenotype characteristics. Any major changes in the numerical value or structure is a cause for medical condition. For ease in studies, similar looking chromosome pairs are lined up in a proper fashion, along with their respective numbers, which is referred to as karyotype. Various researches in human genetics are ongoing to find out the solutions for chromosome related medical conditions.

A chromosome, by definition, is a threadlike strand of DNA in a cell nucleus that carries genes, the units of heredity in a linear order. Human beings have 22 chromosome pairs and a pair of sex chromosomes. Apart from genes, the chromosomes also contain regulatory elements and nucleotide sequences. They house the DNA-bound proteins, which control the functions of the DNA. Interestingly, the word chromosome originated from the Greek word, 'chrome' meaning colour. Chromosomes got their name owing to their property of being stained by dyes. The structure and nature of chromosomes varies across different kinds of organisms. Human chromosomes have always been a subject of interest for the researchers working in genetics. The wide range of factors that human chromosomes determine, the abnormalities they are responsible for and their complex nature have always invited interest of many. Let us look at some interesting facts about the human chromosomes.

Facts About Human Chromosomes

Human cells have 23 pairs of nuclear chromosomes. A chromosome is made up of a DNA molecule that contains genes. A chromosomal DNA molecule contains three nucleotide sequences, which are required for replication. On staining the chromosomes, the banded structure of the mitotic chromosomes becomes apparent. Each band contains numerous DNA nucleotide pairs.

Human beings are sexually reproducing species and have diploid somatic cells having two sets of chromosomes. One set is inherited from the mother while the other one from the father. As against the body cells, the reproductive cells have a single set of chromosomes. The crossover between chromosomes results in the creation of new chromosomes. The newly created chromosomes are not inherited from any single parent. This brings about the fact that not all of us exhibit traits that are directly derived from one of our parents!

There are 24 distinct human chromosomes out of which 22 are autosomal chromosomes and the remaining two are sex-determining chromosomes. The autosomal human chromosomes are numbered from 1 to 22 in the decreasing order of their size. Every individual has two sets of the 22 chromosomes, *X* chromosome from the mother and an *X* or a *Y* chromosome from the father.

An abnormality in the content of the chromosomes of a cell can cause certain genetic disorders in human beings. Chromosomal abnormalities in human beings are often responsible for the appearance of the genetic disorder in their children. Those with chromosomal abnormalities are often only the carriers of the disorder while their children actually exhibit the disorders.

Chromosomal aberrations are caused by a variety of factors namely, deletion or duplication of a part of a chromosome, the inversion, which is the reversal of direction of a chromosome or a translocation wherein a part of a chromosome breaks off to attach to some other chromosome.An extra copy of chromosome 21 is responsible for the very well known genetic disorder that is known as the Down's syndrome. The trisomy of chromosome 18 results in the Edwards syndrome that may cause death in infancy.

The deletion of a part of the fifth chromosome leads to a genetic disorder known as 'cri du chat', meaning 'cry of a cat'. The human beings affected by this disorder show a cat-like crying in childhood and are often mentally retarded.

The disorders caused by sex chromosomes include the Turner syndrome wherein female sexual characteristics are present but underdeveloped, the Triple-X syndrome in girls and the XXY syndrome in boys, both causing dyslexia in the affected individuals.

Chromosomes were first discovered in plants. Van Beneden's monograph on the fertilized eggs of a roundworm, led the research further. Later in time, August Weismann proclaimed that the germ line was different from the soma and he discovered that the cell nucleus housed the hereditary material. He also proposed that fertilization results in a new combination of chromosomes.

These discoveries were cornerstones in the field of genetics. Researchers have achieved a sufficient amount of knowledge of human chromosomes and genes but there is still a lot to be discovered.

DNA Replication Enzymes

Continuity of life is made possible due to inheritance of genetic material by every new generation of organisms. Every family has certain traits inherited from their ancestors. How does biological inheritance work to transmit genetic information down the generations? It is very important to know about this if we aim to understand human genetics. It is made possible by the process of DNA replication. Here we can briefly explain the process of DNA replication and then talk about the role played by the prime DNA replication enzymes.

What is DNA Replication?

Before we talk about the prime enzymes involved in DNA replication, let me explain the process itself and how it works. The DNA molecule contains all the genetic information to create an entire organism. It is the blueprint according to which every biological function occurs. For this genetic information to be transmitted from one generation to the other, it needs to be replicated during cell division, so that every new cell formed carries its identical copy. This process is monitored and controlled by the DNA replication enzymes. Today DNA research has revealed intricate details of how the genetic code is copied or duplicated during cell division.

DNA molecule has a double helix structure with two strands of nucleotides coiled together and held in place by a Ribose sugar-Phosphate backbone. Each strand is made up of a series of nucleotides called Adenine (*A*), Guanine (*G*), Thymine (*T*), Cytosine (*C*). These are the four letters using which the entire genetic code is written. The order of nucleotides on both strands is complementary as Adenine only binds with Thymine and Cytosine only binds with Guanine.

To put in simple words, during the DNA replication process, the DNA double helix is uncoiled (by breakage of hydrogen bonds), each strand is separated and using them as templates, new DNA molecules are created that are exact copies of the original one. DNA replication steps involve the forking of DNA helix, separation of strands and finally addition of complementary nucleotide bases from the template strands to form new DNA molecules. The process is very complex involving an elaborate mechanism to carry out DNA repair and proofreading to ensure accuracy.

Prime DNA Replication Enzymes in Eukaryotes

Now that you have a rough idea of what DNA duplication or replication is, let me talk about the prime DNA replication enzymes in cells that are involved in the replication process. There are many enzymes involved in DNA replication due to the complex nature of the whole process. Here are the main DNA replication enzymes and their functions in eukaryotic cells, during cell division.

Helicase: DNA replication begins at places called origins, within the DNA molecule and the creation of replication forks. The process of strand separation is made possible because of the the enzyme Helicase which separates the two strands using the energy that is derived from ATP hydrolysis.

DNA Primase: One of the most crucial DNA replication enzymes is DNA Primase. After the DNA strands are separated, to begin the creation of new DNA molecules, through addition of complementary bases to the templates, a short RNA segment, called a 'primer' is required. These primers are synthesized by DNA primase enzymes, thus initiating the DNA replication process. That is why DNA Primase is one of the most important DNA replication enzyme.

DNA Polymerase: The most important DNA replication enzymes, that carry out the main task of aligning the complementary bases with template strands of 'unzipped' DNA, are the DNA polymerases. They are a large family of enzymes that carry out the task of adding complementary base nucleotides by reading the template strands. Besides the task of elongating the DNA molecule, they also carry out DNA proofreading and repair.

Exonuclease (DNA Polymerase I): The main function of Exonucleases like DNA polymerase I is to remove the RNA primer segments from the template strand. It is always involved in the 'Search and Remove' operation of RNA primers.

DNA Ligase: While Helicase works to unwind the DNA molecule, DNA Ligase is the DNA replication enzyme that binds the DNA fragments together by addition of phosphates in the gaps that remain in the phophate-ribose sugar backbone.

These DNA replication enzymes are the crucial parts of replication assembly line. The precision with which every single segment of the complementary strand is aligned is mind boggling. No man-made assembly line can match the efficiency, detailing and brilliance of the DNA replication mechanism that makes biological inheritance possible.

DNA is known as the 'blueprint of life'. It was discovered by James Watson, a biologist from Indiana University and Fransis Crick, a physicist. The duo worked at the Cavendish Lab in Cambridge, England on the structure of DNA. With a lot of hurdles and difficulties, they managed to announce to the world, that they had 'found the secret of life'. This secret of life is what we all know as DNA. This molecule undergoes DNA replication process. Thus, DNA replication results in two DNA molecules. This article will cover eukaryotic DNA replication steps and prokaryotic replication steps. But, first let us understand the structure of DNA. Know more on who discovered DNA.

Structure of DNA

DNA (Deoxyribonucleic acid) is a double stranded structure, that has many chains of genetic matter in the form of chromosomes. There are two complementary strands that form a double helix. The two strands of DNA run anti-parallel to each other. One strand runs in the 5′ ? 3′ direction and the other in the parallel direction of 3′ ? 5′ direction. Each strand has a 5′ phosphate end and a 3′ hydroxyl end. The backbone of DNA molecule is the deoxyribose sugar. There are 5 carbons that are numbered 1′, 2′, 3′, 4′ and 5′, to help them to be distinguished from the atoms of purine and pyrimidine rings. The backbone of DNA is formed by the deoxyribose sugar and a phosphate group along with the base. The DNA twists at specific lengths due to the bonding angles of the DNA backbone molecules. This forms a helical structure instead of a straight ladder. The steps of the twisted ladder are made by the base pairs.

The Base Pairs of DNA

The monomer unit of a DNA is called a nucleotide, that consists of a 5-carbon sugar, that is, deoxyribose, a nitrogen attached to the sugar and a phosphate group. There are four types of nucleotide molecules in the DNA structure that differ only in the nitrogenous base. These four nucleotides are as follows:

- Adenine
- Guanine

- Cytosien
- Thymine

The first letter of the nucleotide name is used as an abbreviation for the entire name. Adenine and Guanine are purines and form the larger base pairs in DNA. Cytosine and Thymine form the smaller base pair and are known as pyrimidines. These nucleotides are the base pairs that form hydrogen bonds with the complementary base on the other strand of DNA. Adenine forms a double bond with thymine (*A* = *T*) and cytosine forms a triple bond with guanine (C = *G*)

This was the basic DNA structure. Now let us move on to our main topic of DNA replication steps. The eukaryotic DNA replication steps differ from the prokaryotic DNA replication steps. Both the complementary strands of DNA contain genetic information that is required for the development of a new cell or organism. These two strands serve as templates for the reproduction of the complementary strand. During DNA replication process, the template strand is conserved entirely, with a new strand assembled with the help of nucleotides. This DNA replication process is therefore called as semi-conservative replication. Thus, a double stranded DNA molecule is manufactured, that is identical to the previous strands. This mechanism is fool-proof as there is proofreading and error checking process, to make sure there are minimum errors. Read more on human genetics.

Difference Between the Eukaryotic and Prokaryotic DNA Replication Steps

As mentioned earlier, the eukaryotic DNA replication steps and the prokaryotic DNA replication steps have a different mechanism. The eukaryotic DNA replication steps are more complex than the prokaryotic DNA replication steps. Eukaryotic DNA is found in all complex organisms which includes plants and animals, where as the prokaryotic DNA is present in 'simple' organisms like bacteria and cyanobacteria. The eukaryotic DNA is always present in combination with histone proteins and the prokaryotic DNA is a simple duplex that does not contain histones (that is, basic proteins). In the prokaryotic DNA replication steps, the DNA is replicated during the interval between the cell divisions. The eukaryotic DNA replication steps are highly regulated and the process takes place during the '*S*' phase of the cell cycle, that precedes mitosis or meiosis

DNA Replication Process

DNA replication process is a very complex process, that requires many proteins to act together. These proteins known as replication proteins, are clustered together in the cell and that unit of the cell can be called as the 'Replication Factory'. Here the DNA replication, results in two DNA molecules. The DNA replication proteins each have a specific function in the production of new DNA strand. The six proteins arranged in a ring shape known as Helicase, unwind the double stranded DNA helix into single strands. The tetramers, that is, the single standed binding proteins, cover the single-standed DNA. This prevents the DNA stands from re-annealing and forming the double stranded molecule. The RNA polmerase known as primase, synthesizes short RNA primers that initiate the DNA replication process. DNA polymerase threads the nucleotides together, forming a DNA strand. The DNA polymerase is held on to the DNA strand during the DNA replication step, by an accessory protein called the sliding clamp. 'RNAse H' helps in removing the RNA primers that initiate the DNA strand synthesis. The long continuous DNA strand is created by the linking of short stretches of DNA by DNA ligase. Know more on difference between DNA and RNA.

The Replication Fork

The replication fork is a structure that is formed during the DNA replication process. The fork is made with the action of helicase, that breaks the hydrogen bonds, that hold the two DNA strands together. This results in a structure that has two branching 'prongs' of a single stand DNA each.

Synthesis of New Strands

The two single DNA strands act as templates individually, that are used for producing two complementary DNA strands. The double helix consists of two anti-parallel DNA strands with complementary 5' to 3' strands. The polymerase enzymes synthesize nucleic acid strands only in the 5' ? 3' direction. It hooks the 5' phosphate group of an incoming nucleotide onto the 3' hydroxyl group at the end of the growing nucleic acid chain. Thus, the chain grows on to the extension of the 3' hydroxyl group and the strand synthesis proceeds in the 5' to 3' direction. DNA polymerase cannot begin synthesizing the DNA strand initially. It needs a nucleic chain in the beginning to begin copying the strand. Thus, RNA polymerase called primase, copies the first short stretch of the DNA strand. Thus, creating a complementary RNA segment, that is 60 nucleotides long and known as a primer. This gives the DNA polymerase the required platform to begin copying the DNA strand. It begins at the 3' end of the RNA primer and, with the reference from the old DNA strand, it synthesis the new complementary DNA strand. Two simple DNA replication enzymes are required for each parental DNA strand. The two polymerase enzymes move in opposite direction of the two strands.

During the synthesis, only one polymerase remains on the DNA template and copies the DNA in a continuous strand. The other polymerase copies only a short stretch of DNA, before running into the primer of the initially sequenced fragment. Thus, it needs to release the DNA strand and slide further up stream and start the extension of another RNA primer. The sliding clamp holds the DNA in its place as it moves through the DNA replication process.

The strand that is synthesized continuously is called the leading strand and the strand that is synthesized in short pieces is called the lagging strand. The short pieces of synthesized DNA, that make up the lagging strand, are called the Okazaki fragments.

Synthesis of the Lagging Strand

The lagging strand is the DNA strand of the replication fork, that is opposite to the leading strand. It is synthesized in the opposite direction, that is, 5′ to 3′ instead of the 3′ end as in the leading strand. The DNA polymerase cannot synthesize the strand 5′ ? 3′ as explained above. Thus, the strand is synthesized in short fragments forming a lagging strand known as the Okazaki fragment. Primase builds RNA primers in short bursts over the lagging strand, which is synthesized in the 5′ ? 3′ by DNA polymerase. The RNA primers are removed and new deoxyribonucleotides are added to the gaps, where the RNA was present. These strands are joined by DNA ligase, thus, completing the synthesizis of lagging strand.

Note: The removal of RNA fragments from the strands, have different mechanism in eukarytotic DNA replication steps and prokaryotic DNA replication steps.

Synthesis of the Leading Strand

The DNA strand that is read in the 3′ ? 5′ and synthesized in the 5′ ? 3′ direction continuously, is known as the leading strand. The DNA polymerase III synthesis the DNA using the 3′- OH group, that is donated by the single RNA primer. The DNA replication steps continue in the direction of the replication fork, in a continuous manner

Steps in DNA Replication

Now, that we have understood the basis of the DNA replication and the functions of the simple DNA replication enzymes, let us go through the DNA replication steps in action.

- The double helix structure is unwound by the helciase enzyme exposing two single stranded DNAs. This creates a replication fork, onto which DNA replication process occurs simultaneously on each fork. The proteins that are involved in the DNA replication process are collected in one location of the cell. This shows that the proteins do not move along the length of DNA, but the DNA is fed through the protein factory or area just like a film is fed into a projector.

- ❖ The single-stranded binding proteins (SSBs) cover the DNA strands and thus, preventing them from annealing into a double strand. These SSBs are easily moved by the DNA polymerase enzyme.
- ❖ The original DNA strand is used as a template to synthesize the DNA strand in the 5' ? 3' direction with the help of an extension formed by RNA primer. DNA polymerase can synthesize the strand in 5' ? 3' only, thus, one strand is synthesized in short bursts, that is joined together later on.
- ❖ RNAse H and DNA polymerase I (exonuclease) recognizes the RNA polymers that are bound to the DNA template and removes the primers by RNA hydrolysis.
- ❖ The gaps formed due to hydrolysis of RNA are filled in by the DNA polymerase.
- ❖ The DNA pieces or nicks are filled with deoxyribonucleotides and joined together by the enzyme ligase, thus, completing the DNA replication process.

The human DNA is up to 80 million base pair long in a chromosome. Thus, the DNA is unwound at multiple places along its length and DNA replication steps are carried out simultaneously at many places.

Fact File: The human DNA is copied at about 50 base pairs per second. The multiple location of DNA replication process takes about 1 hour to complete. If this were not the case, then it would take about a month to finish replicating the entire DNA strand!

The DNA replication process is almost error free with the help of DNA polymerase and other simple DNA replication enzymes, that proofread the nucleotides being added to the strand. If the nucleotides are not found to be complementary, then they are removed and a new nucleotide is synthesized. Thus, creating an error free DNA strand

Fact File: A billion nucleotides have less than one mistakes. This means that copying 100 dictionaries with 1000 pages word to word, page to page and symbol to symbol, with only one mistake!

This is all about the DNA replication steps, involved in copying a new DNA strand. A lot of DNA research and DNA sequencing has been carried out to know these minute processes in a cell. The DNA replication process is essential for the survival of all life forms. DNA replication steps occur during the inter-phase and are copied before cell division. Specialized cells like the muscles and nerve cells do not divide, thus, there is no DNA replication process carried out here. DNA is a marvelous coding chip, that contains all the information required for the function of a cell and the organisms. Nature has thought of every detail that helps in the growth of a species. This error free factory of nature, is one of the unmatched manufacturing units, that help produce organisms of the highest quality.

DNA molecules, or deoxyribonucleic acid molecules, are the unique molecules which possess the ability of replicating themselves in a process referred to as DNA replication. It is one of the most important mechanisms in life cells. The complex process of DNA replication involves various biochemical reactions, enzymes, specialized proteins, etc. Before we move on to the actual working process, let's have a brief look at DNA replication. Read more on mitochondrial DNA.

DNA Replication

DNA replication is a process wherein copies of DNA molecules are produced within the cell nucleus. This replication process is vital because it facilitates the transfer of genetic information from one generation to another. DNA possesses the genetic information for the cell, and DNA replication process just helps in duplicating this information, so that the information transfer continues from generation to generation. The process has the ability to produce exact replicas of the said genetic material. So how does this overall process of DNA replication take place?

What is the DNA Replication Process?

Like all other cellular activities in living organisms, even DNA replication process requires specialized proteins. As one of the very first DNA replication process steps, helicase, a specialized protein in the cells, facilitates the splitting of the two strands of DNA which make up the double helix. Often found in a coiled state and being highly stable, it is a bit difficult to split the DNA double helix. The splitting part is facilitated by DNA gyrases, which relaxes and uncoil the DNA molecule. While this uncoiling is being carried out by DNA gyrases, another enzyme starts unzipping the molecule, by breaking the hydrogen bonds between the base pairs.

This is followed by binding between a molecule of DNA polymerase to one of the split strands of DNA. The free nucleotides in the nucleus pairs with the matching bases of the split strands. These nucleotides are eventually joined together in order to form a new complementary strand of DNA. A single-strand binding proteins helps in binding the separated strands and facilitates DNA replication. This results in producing two copies of the DNA molecule, each featuring one new strand and one strand from the original molecule. The replication process is semi-conservative, as half part of each molecule is new, while the other half is conserved from the original DNA molecule. Read more on DNA replication steps.

Replication Control Mechanism

Basically, there are two DNA replication control mechanisms – one positive and one negative. Each replication site, referred to as 'origins', has to be bound by a set of proteins to facilitate the initiation of DNA replication.

This set of proteins, referred to as Origin Recognition Complex, remains attached to the DNA molecules throughout the entire process of replication. Another set of proteins, referred to as licensing factors, is also required for initiation of replication. When the replication process is complete, these proteins are destructed in order to prevent further replication cycles.

- ❖ You may also like to read more about DNA
- ❖ DNA paternity testing
- ❖ DNA testing
- ❖ Differece between DNA and RNA

This was the basic information about the replication process of DNA in the cells of various living organisms. DNA replication process is undoubtedly a complex process, which requires deep understanding about various scientific concepts and DNA research. To make it more simple, in a DNA replication process, two complementary strands forming a DNA molecule are separated and used as templates to produce new strands by nucleotides combining to their complementary bases.

Genetic Predisposition

Genetic predisposition, also called as genetic susceptibility, is defined as the effect of gene that influences the phenotype expression of an individual, including the susceptibility to certain diseases and disorders. As we already know, genetic composition is directly responsible for the physical attributes of an organism. Unlike this genotypic effect, the affectation of genetic predisposition can be altered or changed with respect to environmental factors. In contrary to this, environmental predisposition refers to influencing the phenotype by external conditions.

Genetic Predisposition — Explained

In medical science, genetic predisposition is evaluated to correlate the possibility of diseases developing in an individual and disposition of the genes to the particular health problems. Like for instance, an individual having a predisposition for schizophrenia has an increased risk of manifesting this psychotic disorder than the general population. However, it doesn't mean that he or she will surely get the condition. The main approach used for identifying genetic predisposition is none other than genetic testing and screening. For your understanding, genetic predisposition of various cases are highlighted below:

Genetic Predisposition to Obesity

Go through the probable causes of obesity and you will come across genetic predisposition as one of the factors responsible along with diet and lifestyle habits. In a study conducted in Boston University Medical School, it is found that a slight alteration in the gene (INSIG2) is the primary reason for obese propensity. As this particular gene undergoes changes, it affects fat production in the body, thereby increasing the risk of becoming overweight or obese. Similar to this, some people are genetically predisposed to remain slim.

Genetic Predisposition to Addiction

It is suggested that approximately 50 per cent cases of alcohol addiction are caused due to genetic predisposition to alcoholism. The remaining 50 per cent are because of poor coping skills. Keeping it in statistical terms, the offspring of drug addicts are eight times more prone to become addicted than others. Supporting this statement, Dr. Nora Volkow, the director of national institute on drug abuse (NIDA), claimed that some individuals are genetically predisposed to addiction.

Genetic Predisposition to Depression

When it comes to treatment of major depression problems, the option lies in identifying the underlying causes and preventing them. But, the main query that lingers in the minds of physician is the genetic basis of depression. A genetic research of identical twins concluded that if one of them is depressed, the other person has 50 per cent chances of getting depressed. No doubt, the gene responsible for triggering depression symptoms is identified. But, it differs from one report to another. Thus, it is still not clear as to which gene leads to depression.

Genetic Predisposition to Disease

Apart from genetic disorders, genetic predisposition to cancer, diabetes and osteoarthritis have been studied on a global scale. It is found that a person having a medical history of diabetes, either in first-degree relative (parents or siblings) or second-degree relative (uncle, aunt, cousins) is more likely to develop this blood sugar problem than others. Likewise, an individual with a genetic predisposition to lung cancer should refrain from smoking to reduce risk of developing lung carcinoma in the later stages of life. According to scientists, genetic predisposition has both positive and negative effects. The good point is inheritance of intelligence, strong mental ability and specific talents from parents to their offspring. Whereas, tendency to develop mental disorders and medical conditions is the downside story of genetic disposition. In the concluding note, studying human genetics and identifying disposition towards a disease will surely help an individual in minimizing the risk of developing it in future.

Have you ever wondered, why is it that your little brother can roll his tongue and you just can't seem to roll yours? Or have you been wondering how come you have freckles, but your best friend doesn't? My dad has straight hair and my mom has really curly hair. And I was born with, a combination of both, wavy hair! Is it a matter of co-incidence or was there some kind of mixing happening somewhere? Was this mixing that gave me hair that was in combination of my parents hair type? Well, there was plenty of mix and match happening down at the genetic level. This process of gene pooling is what helps in expression of the dominant and recessive traits in humans. Let us go into the details of some of the recessive and dominant traits in humans.

What are the Dominant and Recessive Traits in Humans?

One of the most important principles that governs life is inheritance of genes. There are over 200 traits that are transmitted from generation to generation in humans. These interesting aspects of human genetics are known as hereditary traits. These hereditary traits include the dominant and recessive traits in humans. Most of the genes are transmitted in the Mendelian pattern and a few are transmitted through the non-Mendelian pattern that includes: co-dominance, sex-linked genes and polygenes. You can read more on list of genetic disorders.

The physical traits are those that are expressed and what makes every individual an 'individual'. These genes reside on specific segments of the DNA. Each gene is grouped to form a chromosome and each chromosome is found in the nucleus of the cell. There are two copies of each gene present in an individual's body with the exception of eggs and sperms. These two gene copies include one copy of the gene from the mother and one copy from the father. Thus, we see some of our physical traits are similar to our mother and some match our father's traits. You can read more on genetic engineering in humans.

There are two or more variations in most of the genes called alleles. An individual can inherit same pair of alleles or two different pairs of alleles. When there are two different alleles, they are expressed in a different way. The trait that is expressed in case of two different alleles, gives rise to the dominant and recessive traits in humans. When a dominate allele is present, it is always observed that the dominant trait is expressed. The recessive trait is observed only in case there are two recessive alleles present.

It is generally believed that the dominant alleles are the most common traits observed in a population. However, this is not a complete fact. Many times the alleles may be dominant, but the allele for expression of a trait may be recessive. Thus, many times the dominant trait is not expressed in an individual. Let me explain this inheritance pattern in the following examples.

Common Dominant and Recessive Traits in Humans

These are some of the common dominant and recessive traits in humans that can be easily observed in people around you.

Widow's Peak

A widow's peak or the mid-digital hairline is due to expression of the gene for hairline. This gene has two alleles, one for widow's peak and one for straight hairline. The widow's peak allele is dominant and the straight allele is recessive. When two widow's peak alleles are present, the individual will have a peak. Then one widow's peak and one straight allele is present, it will give rise to expression of a peak. However, when there are two recessive genes, that is, straight hairline alleles, the expression of the trait is a straight hairline.

Bent Pinkie

You can try and bend your pinkie finger inwards towards your ring finger or fourth finger. If you are able to do so, it means you have inherited the dominant version of the gene that causes the distal segment of the pinkie to bend.

Crossing of Thumbs

You need to observe the position of your thumbs in a relaxed interlocking of fingers. Do you find your left thumb crossing your right thumb? If yes, then you probably have inherited 1 or 2 copies of the dominate gene. In case of 2 recessive genes inherited, you will find your right thumb placed over your left thumb.

These were just a few examples of dominant and recessive traits in humans. Let us see some more of these traits in the following list of dominant and recessive traits in humans.

List of Dominant and Recessive Traits in Humans

These dominant and recessive traits in humans are commonly observed in individuals. The following list of dominant and recessive traits in humans will help answer the questions mentioned in the beginning of the article. You can read more on human genetics.

Earlobe Attachment

Some people have their earlobes attached to the side of the head and some people have free earlobes. This is due to a gene that is dominant for unattached earlobes and recessive in case of attached earlobes.

Rolling of Tongue

If you can roll the lateral edges of your tongue together, then this means you have inherited a dominant trait. Those who are unable to do so are expressing inheritance of recessive gene for tongue rolling.

Cleft Chin

People who have a cleft chin have inherited a dominant gene and those with smooth chin have recessive gene.

Dimples

Have you fallen for the cute dimples of Brad Pitt? Well, Brad Pitt and people all over the world with dimples are expressing the dominant gene for dimples. Whereas, people without dimples have recessive genes.

Handedness

The gene for right handedness is dominant and the gene for left hand is recessive. Thus, majority of the people have inherited the dominant gene resulting in right handedness.

Natural Curly Hair

The gene for naturally curly hair is dominant and the gene for straight hair is recessive. (Does this mean I have one dominant and one recessive gene that resulted in my wavy hair? Interesting.) You can read more on inherited genetic diseases.

Freckles

All those with freckles, you have inherited at least one pair of dominant gene for freckles. Those without freckles have inherited two recessive genes for freckles. You can read more on genetic disorders in humans.

Allergies

People with allergies may have inherited the gene for allergy from at least one of the parent. It is seen that a parent with allergies has a chance that one of four of their children may develop allergy. The chances of child inheriting allergy from a parent is about 25 per cent and the risk increases if both parents have allergies.

Colour Blindness

Colour blindness is a genetic disorder that is seen due to presence of a recessive allele located on the *X* chromosome. There are two *X* chromosome in women and one of them usually carries an allele for normal vision. In men, there is only one *X* chromosome and if they carry an allele for colourblindness, they will express this trait. This is the reason that more number of men are colourblind as compared to women. You can read more on colour blindness genetics.

These were just a few dominant and physical traits in humans. Other dominant and recessive traits in humans include:

Dominant Trait in Humans	Recessive
A blood type	O blood type
Abundant body hair	Little body hair
Astigmatism	Normal vision
B blood type	O blood type
Baldness (in male)	Not bald
Broad lips	Thin lips
Broad nose	Narrow nose
Dwarfism	Normal growth
Hazel or green eyes	Blue or gray eyes
High blood pressure	Normal blood pressure

(Contd...)

Large eyes	Small eyes
Migraine	Normal
Mongolian Fold	No fold in eyes
Nearsightedness	Normal vision
Rh factor (+)	No factor (Rh -)
Second toe longest	First or big toe longest
Short stature	Tall stature
Six fingers	Five fingers normal
Webbed fingers	Normal fingers
Tone deafness	Normal tone hearing
White hair streak	Normal hair

These were some of the dominant and recessive traits in humans. Every physical, emotional, mental and health trait exhibited by an individual is all due to gene expression. Whether one wants to or does not want, genes are inherited by default. One can never know what traits a baby will inherit from which parent. The genes contain the secrete of life, that is unravelled only after a baby is born. I hope this article has helped you learn and understand some of the dominant and recessive traits in humans.

CHAPTER 16

Point Mutations

Mutation is defined as an alteration in the nucleotide sequence of DNA (deoxyribonucleic acid) of an organism. The structure of DNA consists of nitrogenous bases (purines and pyrimidines), glucose and phosphate. Purine consists of adenine (*A*) and guanine (*G*) bases, whereas pyrimidine bases are cytosine (C) and thymine (*T*). The bases are arranged as codons (three bases) that describe the coding of proteins for expression of cells. Mutation occurs when the sequence of nitrogenous base is changed, either due to copying errors during the replication or an exposure to mutagens such as chemicals, pollution, cigarette smoke, radiation and sunlight. The outcome of mutation is a change in the genetic message coded by the gene.

Types of Mutation

In general, mutation is classified into two types based on the cells that are getting affected, namely, germ line and somatic. In the former case, mutation occurs in the reproductive cells (egg and sperm), which is then inherited from the parents to the offspring. This germ line mutation is responsible for causing hereditary diseases and/or genetic disorders. Somatic mutation, on the other hand, takes place in body cells like skin. It is not inherited to the descendants.

Depending upon the effect of mutation on the structure of DNA, mutation can be further divided into several types viz. substitution (exchanging base between two DNA strands), insertion (extra base is inserted in a DNA strand), deletion (loss of base pairs), inversion (reverse of base sequence) and frame-shift (insertion and deletion of one or more base pairs). Let's discuss in brief about single-base substitution or point mutation.

Point Mutations

When a single base in the nucleotide sequence is replaced by another, then it is known as point mutation. Point mutations also include insertion and/or deletion of a single base in the DNA strand. Usually, they are caused due to error in DNA replication. At times, point mutations occur after exposure to mutagens like heat and radiation.

Point mutations can be either transitions or transversions. In the former case, a purine base (adenine, guanine) is substituted by another purine or a pyrimidine base (cytosine, thymine) is replaced by another pyrimidine. In transversion type of point mutations, purine is substituted by pyrimidine or vice versa. Transition point mutation is more common than transversion type.

The effects of point mutation can vary depending upon the site of mutation on the gene. If point mutation occurs in the coding sequence of DNA or exon, then the protein coded by the altered gene is changed. In case of point mutation in the non-coding sequence or intron, it may result in the change in RNA splicing, which in turn, affects the coding of gene.

Some other possible outcomes of point mutations include a failure of DNA transcription (conversion of messenger RNA to proteins), alteration of regulatory responses and other genetic changes. Hence, based on the functional changes of the gene, point mutations are divided into three types, namely, nonsense (failure of expression), missense (base code for a different protein) and silent (no significant change). The diseases like sickle cell anaemia and thalassaemia are caused due to missense mutation in the coding sequence of a gene.

A genetic disorder is a disease or illness caused by different genes. It's basically caused by variation of a gene or an alteration of a gene called mutation. So to explain in a simple statement, genetic disorders are illnesses caused by abnormalities of the genes or chromosomes. Medical facts claim that most dangerous diseases have a genetic aspect. Life threatening diseases like cancer where cells undergo a drastic change are caused by mutation in a single gene or a group of genes in a person's cells. There is no appropriate explanation on what causes genetic disorders in children, it can be due to exposure to harmful radiation or even frequent smoking.

Most cases of genetic disorders in children are due to inheritance. A mutated gene is passed down in every generation and the new born inherits the gene which leads to genetic disorders. However, it has also been observed that in various types of genetic disorders the main issue begins with the extra number of groups of genes called chromosomes.

Rare Genetic Disorders in Children

Seeing a child born with a genetic disorder is disheartening for any family. It becomes more difficult when you realize that your child is suffering from a rare genetic disorder. To understand the situation better and also know the diagnosis it's very necessary that you have the basic information on rare genetic diseases and disorders in children.

LMBBS

LMBBS or Laurence-Moon-Bardet-Biedl Syndrome is the main cause of extra toes or fingers, retinal degeneration, behavioural problems, various muscular disorders, obesity, and mental and verbal delays. Children suffering from LMBBS are often victims of stunted growth. The diagnosis of LMBBS focuses on making the child get over his social fears and making sure that he/she gets the required help needed for vision impairment and speech disorders. If you have a child or know someone suffering from LMBBS, seek help from The Laurence-Moon-Bardet-Biedl Society which is specially designed to help out children suffering from this rare genetic disorder.

Trisomy 18

One of the most dangerous inherited genetic diseases, Trisomy 18 occurs when a baby has an extra number 18 chromosome. Children born with this condition do not live more than a year but some are fortunate to live longer. Babies born with Trisomy 18 have very low birth weight and they have a difficult time breathing and swallowing. Babies who can suck survive but this genetic mutation is incurable. It's diagnosis focuses on teaching children basic gross motor skills. To make sure they maintain a healthy weight nutritionists often help babies suffering from Trisomy 18. To know more information on this disease parents can reach out to the Trisomy 18 Foundation.

Fragile X Syndrome

The meaning of this disease is there in it's name. Children suffering from Fragile *X* Syndrome suffer from a damaged or a broken *X* chromosome. The damaged chromosome is not able to create the protein it's supposed to make and this causes mental retardation, mood disorders and anxiety, autism and unusual speech patterns. Kids suffering rrom Fragile *X* Syndrome also have physical symptoms like flat feet, expendable joints, high palate and a long face. Treatment includes early training sessions which helps them to talk and also improve their brain condition. To know more, get in touch with The National Fragile *X* Foundation.

Tuberous Sclerosis

TSC or Tuberous Sclerosis starts the growth of benign tumors in the vital organs of the body. These tumors causes a host of problems like seizures, developmental delays and irregular behavioural patterns. Doctors focus on the removal of tumors and on administering of seizure medication. Severe TSC can cause mental impairment but it has also been observed that children with mild symptoms of Tuber Sclerosis live a normal life. For more advise and support you can go The National Tuberous Sclerosis Alliance.

Common Genetic Disorders in Children

Children born with genetic abnormalities are either born with less or more number of chromosomes. Here's a list of the most common genetic diseases that affect children globally.

- Down Syndrome (Children with one extra chromosome)
- Turner Syndrome (Common in girls, they have one X chromosome and are missing the second sex chromosome)
- Klinefelter Syndrome (Found only in boys, they have one Y chromosome and two X chromosomes)
- Angelman Syndrome (A missing gene segment on chromosome 15, this syndrome is inherited from the mother)
- Prader-Willi Syndrome (Another missing gene on chromosome 15, but this time this disorder is inherited from the father)
- Duchenne Muscular Dystrophy (Only found in boys, X chromosome is missing which means shortage of essential protein)
- Cystic Fibrosis (Kids suffering from CF have defective glands that produce large amounts of thick mucus which creates problems in effective breathing and digestion)

❖ Tay-Sachs Disease (Kids suffering from Tay-Sachs Disease suffer from a gene defect of the central nervous system. This defect prevents the formation of an enzyme which helps break down fatty substances in brain cells)

❖ Phenylketonuria (Children suffering from PKU have problems with the liver as it prevents the liver from producing an enzyme which breaks down phenylalanine. This accumulation of phenylalanine can prove toxic to the brain)

So these were some of the rare, and common genetic disorders in children. Scientists have still not been able to identify what triggers genetic disorders in humans but they often blame the unhealthy lifestyle which most of us lead. So to be free of all the problems and to live a long and happy life, it's advised that you have a balanced diet and follow an exercise programme religiously.

Aspects of Human Genetics

The fact that human genetics can answer questions related to diseases in human beings, their treatment, the genetic disorders and more importantly the human nature, makes this field interesting. It includes different fields such as classical and clinical genetics and genomics. Human genetics deals with the study of the inheritance pattern in the human beings. The potential uses of human genetics in the study of human nature and its prospective applications in medicine have made it a subjec. of interest for one and all.

Interesting Aspects of Human Genetics

❖ Gregor Mendel studied the inheritance of the traits in living beings. He concluded that inheritance depends upon discrete units known as genes and he came up with a model of inheritance. He deduced that the inheritance of traits follows certain laws. For his significant work in genetics, Mendel is known as the father of genetics.

❖ Inheritance traits in human beings are either autosomal or *X* or *Y* linked. Autosomes are the non-sex chromosomes whereas the *X*-linked and the *Y*-linked genes are found on the sex chromosomes. Let us look at each of them.

- In case of autosomal recessive inheritance, a trait or a disorder is passed on through families. For a recessive trait to show in humans, two copies of that trait are required. Since two copies of the disorder or the trait are needed for its display, it can remain hidden for generations together. Many human beings can be unaware of the fact that they are acting as carriers of the trait or disorder.
- Autosomal dominant inheritance is a pattern wherein a single copy of a trait is sufficient for it to appear in a human being. If one of the parents has this trait, it can be displayed in their children.
- Traits inherited from the sex chromosomes include the *X*-linked and the *Y*-linked inheritance. *X*-linked genes can be autosomal or recessive. Recessive *X*-linked disorders are common among males. As a father passes his *Y* chromosome to his son, *X*-linked traits or disorders are inherited from the maternal side. The expression of *X*-linked traits in the females depends on their zygosity for the trait. When a female is homozygous for a particular trait or disorder, it means that she carries two identical copies of the gene affecting that trait. In case she is heterozygous for a particular disorder, it means that she has two different alleles for that disorder. Homozygous females display *X*-linked disorders while the heterozygous females become carriers for the disorder. *Y*-linked disorders are carried on the *Y* chromosome. As it is present only in males, a *Y*-linked trait is transferred from a father to his son.
- Apart from the nuclear DNA, human beings possess mitochondrial DNA. It is believed that the mitochondria are descended from a proteobacterium, which merged with eukaryotic cells, around two billion years ago. Mitochondrial DNA is about 16 KB long. A human being inherits mitochondria from his/her mother. This

makes it evident that DNA can be used to track a person's maternal lines. Interestingly, in some species like the mussels or insects like the honeybees, paternally inherited mitochondria are observed. A single case of paternal inheritance of mitochondria was reported in humans. But it was associated with infertility.

❖ Genes play a vital role in personality characteristics and human behavior. Facial features are linked to genetic constitution of an individual. A human being inherits the characteristics like facial dimples, colour of the iris, the structure of the earlobe and other such traits through the genes. Attributes such as the overall stature and susceptibility to certain diseases are also inherited genetically.

Human genetics has evolved to a level where we have been able to manipulate the genetic constitution of an embryo to a certain extent through genetic engineering. The knowledge of human genetics has led us to be able to enhance the positive traits in humans while removing the negative ones. The various interesting aspects of human genetics have unfolded the mysteries of the physical and psychological characteristics of humans and opened doors to the betterment of human life.

Human Genetic Engineering

Human genetic engineering is about genetically engineering human beings by modifying their genotypes before birth. The Genotype is the genetic constitution of an individual with respect to a particular character under consideration. This is done to control the traits possessed by the individual after his/her birth.

The cells of our body contain encoded information about the body's growth, structure and functioning in the form of genes. Human genetic engineering aims at decoding this information and applying it to the welfare of mankind.

There are two types of genetic engineering. They are:

- *Somatic modification:* Genes are added to the cells. This can prove to be a cure for diseases caused by defective genes. Somatic modifications cannot be inherited.
- *Germline modification:* In this form of human genetic engineering, genes in the early embryos are changed. The genes modified in this way are inheritable. This is an effective form of genetic engineering, as it results in permanent modifications.

Human genetic engineering can be classified as positive genetic engineering and negative genetic engineering. In the positive type of genetic engineering, the positive traits of individuals are enhanced. This can mean increasing longevity or increasing human capacity. The negative genetic engineering is about introducing the good copy of a certain gene into the cells of a living being. Consequently, the suffering characteristic to genetic diseases can be reduced to a great extent.

In human genetic engineering, the genes or the DNA of a person are changed. This can be used to bring about structural changes in human beings. More importantly, it can be used to introduce the genes for certain positive and desirable traits in embryos. Human genetic engineering can result in finding a permanent cure for many diseases.

There are people with certain exceptional qualities. If the genes responsible for these qualities can be identified, they can be implanted in the early embryos. This can lead to something like 'personalized babies'! Human genetic engineering might progress to such an extent that it will be possible to discover new genes and embed them into unborn babies.

Human Genetic Engineering — The Lighter Side

Gene therapy is one of the most important benefits of human genetic engineering. Over the past decade, gene therapy has succeeded in finding treatments for certain heart diseases. Researchers hope to find cures for all the genetic diseases. This will result in a healthier and more evolved human race.

A future benefit of human genetic engineering is that a fetus with a genetic disorder will be treated before the baby is born. Parents will be able to look forward to a healthy baby. In case of in-vitro fertilization, gene therapy can be used for embryos before they are implanted into the mother.

Genes can be cloned to produce pharmaceutical products of superior quality. Researchers are hopeful about being able to bio-engineer plants or fruits to contain certain drugs.

Human Genetic Engineering — The Darker Side

Firstly, while it seems easy to cure diseases by genetic modifications, gene therapy may manifest side effects. While treating one defect, it may cause another. Any given cell is responsible for many activities and manipulating its genes may not be that easy.

The process of cloning can lead to risking the fundamental factors such as the individuality and the diversity of human beings. Ironically, man will become just another man-made thing!

There are certain social aspects to human genetic engineering. This new form of medical treatment can impose a heavy financial burden on the society. Along with its feasibility, its affordability will also determine its popularity.

Human genetic engineering is a widely growing field. It can work miracles. But its benefits and threats need to be assessed carefully. The potential advantages of the field can come into reality only if the genetic engineering of humans is handled with responsibility.

Index

E

G

H